Anvil New Poets

Anvil New Poets

Edited by Graham Fawcett

Anvil Press Poetry

Published in 1990
by Anvil Press Poetry Ltd
69 King George Street London SE10 8PX

Selection and introduction © Graham Fawcett 1990

This book is published
with financial assistance
from The Arts Council

Designed and composed by Anvil
Photoset in Plantin by Wordstream
Printed in England by
Southampton Book Company

British Library Cataloguing in Publication Data

Anvil new poets.
   I. Poetry in English, 1945–   –Anthologies
   I. Fawcett, Graham 1946–
   821.91408

   ISBN 0 85646 230 6

Contents

Introduction

Every year the Anvil Press is sent hundreds of unsolicited type-scripts of poetry. The average envelope contains thirty poems and a letter asking that they be considered for publication as a book. In time, each one is read. For the last eighteen months of the 1980s, this task was shared with me as an outside reader.

In the first week I came across a thick batch of translations by Michael Smith from the Spanish of Góngora and recommended them without hesitation. Anvil agreed, and will publish them in 1991. This was to be the only whole book I discovered throughout the eighteen months to be accepted by the Press. I went on reading. Out of every hundred poets or so, I found one whose work defied rejection by its quality. When I had ten, discussions with the Anvil editors led to the idea of an anthology to introduce these new poets. All of them have had single poems published in poetry magazines, none a body of work in book form in this country. *Anvil New Poets* is the first collection of its kind in Anvil's twenty-two-year, two hundred-book history.

But what is quality? I had no conscious idea what I was looking for but recognized it when I saw it. With the great poets, like Dante and Shakespeare, it is only when I stop reading to study them that I am aware of form and metre. New poets who have attempted poetry's five-finger exercises, counted their syllables, read and practised metre and rhyme, sonnets, triolets and haiku, even as pastiche, can write from the benefit of having done so, even if they opt out of actually using these models. Others see certain forms or rhythms as an obligatory challenge if their poem is to convince.

Many of the typescripts included poems in which form becomes a straitjacket, metre a relentless thump, and the original idea of the poem is cramped and stressed into a pulp. Where structure is neither a façade nor an effect, I can be drawn into the life the poet is leading (daily life, inner life). If the writing is not self-conscious, I am free to relax and be caught off-guard by the clarity and naturalness of invention, and to trust the integrity of its persuasion and surprise.

In London earlier this year, the Czech poet Miroslav Holub said that he had been meaning for some time to write a poem about the British Museum. This was because every time he went there, he was struck by the same thing. The truly imposing exhibits like the great stone human-headed lions, the mythological wonders, did not attract children or adults anything like as much as a mummy or Peat-Bog Man could. Was there skin under the bandages, they wanted to know, was that funny brown shiny surface stretched over the skeleton of Peat-Bog Man still skin, the same as ours? In other words, an exhibit is wonderful to behold not for its exotic difference, but because of its resemblance to the spectator. This sense of a common lot is what makes the connection. Under their bandages and funny colour, poems need to give a sense of skin.

This helps to explain my resistance to, and distrust of, relentless exotica, the ungrounded dream, in the poetry I have been reading. Vivid imagination and verbal gymnastics can turn poetry into a sanitized circus where the ordinary life-issues are missing, where the acrobat isn't a person, so there's no need to fear for her life.

New poetry's other black hole is introspection. Eliot's insistence that 'the more perfect the artist, the more completely separate in him will be the man who suffers and the mind which creates', comes in handy when you want to write well about yourself. The ten poets in this book manage to set aside their ongoing struggle in order to contemplate it, like a hungry painter sketching his supper. Agony or happiness in the poetry is then not so full of itself that the reader's own cannot easily find room alongside it. Bereavement, for example, wants to be left alone to behave in poetry like the intensely commonplace trauma it also is. Or, as the American poet Marvin Bell used to reel off to his creative writing students at the University of Iowa: 'I don't want any more poems about relationships, I know everything there is to know about relationships, bring me a poem about a glass of water and you'll have told me more about life, love and eternity than you ever could by trying to write about life, love and eternity.'

A poem can be good because it gives a sense of timelessness. It remains a product of its time. Many of the poems in this book were written in the late 1980s. Does it show? Most poems prefer to conjure up special moments which did not make the news, yet at any given time actions and words in the public arena exert pressure on the style and content of personal work. The natural landscape in the late 1980s, for instance, was proved to conceal pitiful new secrets about its health. Could this fact not have undermined our sense of the miracle of renewal from season to season, and so injected lament into our impulse to praise the environment in poems?

Anvil New Poets has the advantage of having been invented by the poets who appear in it. The range and variety of poems in this accidental book increase the impression that my editorial judgement has range and variety, while the fact that I commissioned none of it can only strengthen the validity of this sample of work by poets for each of whom a first book is still in the future, probably not far off, and in one or two cases already promised.

GRAHAM FAWCETT
May 1990

Shirley Bell

WHAT?

Tonight, she has hung up her uniform
– packed away and forgotten as homework –
in a bedroom stamp-albumed with stars.
She paints her face for the friend of a friend,
dabs a Christmas perfume on her wrists.

When they leave the pub, she is wading through
thickening pavements. He says he knows a club
up narrow stairs where she stumbles dimly
to a syrup of voices, smiles, more drinks for her.
He kisses her mouth and holds her elbow tighter.

And it's late now. Shop windows glister
with swan-necked women in pretty clothes
the colour of sweetpapers; he clamps her wrist.
Cars are sliding past like a fairground
golden with headlights, crimson with brakes.

They argue in the underpass. She is begging
for a taxi or a late-night bus. People look away.
Now he has her in streets dark with the emptiness
of houses. Fucks her twice where broken glass winks
in the fizzled moonlight like friends of his in bars.

Home is a long way away. 'What did you expect?'
he says. 'You could hardly call it rape.'

HALF-MADE

His eyes are two blank mirrors;
darkened silver. I can see
my own face in them – as in
the polish of a spoon – my eyes
round, my mouth moving, moving.

When I first held him in my arms
he was milky, indistinct, but
my own son. Though his father
denied him. My breasts were honey;
he closed his eyes to suck.

One morning I woke to the foisted
child, gathered in the crib;
eyes empty. I crept away,
astonished. I was bound and gagged.
Later I heard him singing runic
songs; they wheezed to a baby's wail
when I stood, clay-footed, at his door.
I knew my dreamt child was stolen.

The old mothers came to make 'o'
mouths: 'He'll grow straight, you'll
see.' I heard their thoughts.
They knew him, too. Then the doctor
breathed dark names. He showed me
shadowed pictures in a book, talked
of help and clinics; I knew better.
Outside the leaves were falling.

I know better. Come winter,
I will have my true child back.
I know old magic – how to hold
midsummer dew in glass to pillow
dreams and see my lover's face
– though rue the day I did it. How
to flower the cockerel's crimson
throat and read a future in its bones.

And changelings? You must startle them
to honesty. Now I have water, rising
to a boil; a poker whitened in the
fire's angry heart. And the foisted
child, unblinking, lies and waits.

A WINTER'S TALE

Horse chestnuts corkscrew through
an oriental wood of stooped
rhododendrons. Deflated hedgehog
cases, hollowed out for nuts,
rot softly where the acorns split
their sides. All the gold is dross:
the year beneath their feet is wet,
thickening, the hillside
blotting out what sun there is . . .
The lake snatches drowning paths;

saturated roots wring their hands.
Something's lost, slips away, like
leaves that float their frail canoes
across the water. Now there's a silent
avenue of snow between the trees,
a slow swish of tyres banding
the white with darkened parallels.
There is nothing here, no one here.
Only the lake moves, dribbling at its
thawing shores, at the pillowed banks.

These are wetlands, balanced
on the brim; in December
winter slops over and, enticingly,
the waters run. Now the land-raft
floats upon a hollow, where clouds
criss-cross absence, where birdwings
move through ripples, slowly, slowly . . .
and here is a house of dead babies
where the walls seep disapproval
and children play with bones.

The tree lights wink, cynically.
A television roars with laughter.
Some things they cannot wrap . . .
Beyond the windows pale clouds fume
against a sky 'as heavy as her heart'.
How the screen changes does not change –
Fog sighs off the water's belly,
and weaves above the undertow towards
a red-eyed sun. Frosts salt the lawns.
The cat's fastidious toes are spread.

Theirs is a time to wait. And count
dark pigeons where they knot the wires
that sing their messages across the
fields. Repetitions. Grace notes. Then
spring will fling crook-fingered bracken,
trickle primroses up and down the banks,
mesh the sky with nets and nets of leaves . . .
while that still water sucks and creeps,
continues to display its emptied face,
and tells of absences, of all that's gone.

STUBBLE-BURNING

Spilling hot beads across the field
I balanced the fire on a pitchfork
to shake it out, little by little.

Then it was animal, running from us,
quickly, quickly. Cracking our ears
with the sound of its feet, urgent

through the stubble. Where its black
prints showed, the white smoke thinned,
darkened. And the sky, evasive –

you, too, running ahead of me. 'Think
what you're doing, lad!' Thickened air,
dancing with charred pepper. I would

consume . . . Next there was a slow grey
sky, something soft, with velvet
and violet in it. The stubble blued

and trailed with lines of ash. And in
the dusk white eyes of fire, blinking
at the smoke that stings to tears.

How you turned and said 'not you,
you're too . . . ' You laughed. As if I
couldn't fail to understand. And yet

came spring, the corn half grown, my
tongue flickered on your body. Until
you burned, arching in the tractor ruts.

You asking 'have you met my bit of rough?'
Speculative eyes and laughter, my hands
and feet grown bigger. Something burning.

The sky consumed in black. I stayed behind
and watched the fires, transformed to
chains of party lights across the field.

LADY AND THE LAKE

You wouldn't guess this was a love poem:
think of a lady with a white consumptive face
trailing frost around a winter lake. She could
wear a coat with lots of fur, maybe a muff.
Cameras roll. 'Ice has closed this face.'
Sonorous voice-over. She is dumb. Close in
on the frozen lake. 'It practises deceptions
and invites disaster.' Now she speaks;
such vowels! 'He gives me only this blank mask.'
Now we see her lover's face, lips folded.
He should be in uniform, so give him boots.
'Or a shifting surface where expressions flourish
their confusions.' Now the surrealist touch.
We'll see them both naked. Focus on her tits.
She keeps saying, 'I'm a lake, will pour myself
over you, will swallow you.' He shows his teeth.
I think, perhaps, he's laughing. That's it. Cut.

OUT FOR SUNDAY TEA

It's only a bus ride –
then I'm back in that dusk-dark garden
where martins scream of leaving
and rowan berries splash the path.
My cousin and I are anyone we want.
There's the vinegar taste of salmon,
and the sweet geometry of fruit from tins.
The grown-ups talk and drink their tea
while our eyes prickle into roundness
in the darkening panes. 'Pretend that I'm ... '
But it's almost time to go.
At home, my uniform rustles in the wardrobe.
Stiff and uncompromising,
it knows better who I have to be.

I call back once.
My daughter walks the unfamiliar lawns
and watches her changing face
in a pond that wasn't there. 'Sorry.'
We didn't make the wedding and my cousin's gone.
My aunt displays a hanger; a white discarded dress.
I try to fill it out –
but she could be anyone if I met her now.
We grown-ups talk and drink our tea.

SILVER WEDDING

She has gathered herself up,
with her dress, for this great effort.
The cake is baying at her:
'Happy Anniversary, Mum and Dad!'

His eyes are polished with whisky.
'I always did my best,' he says.
'I always tried to do the proper thing.'

For a moment she, too, tries to see
his watered visions. She looks instead
through years of closing doors at
thirteen hundred Sunday dinners singeing
while his quick ones lingered on;
at the mirror's unkind answers
every time she asks it 'who?';
at her redundant mothering . . .

'Twenty-five happy years!' he says.

It has taken years to reverse
the curve of her lips to this.
Her face is a sag of disappointment,
pains in her side, and prescriptions
'you can collect from the receptionist . . .
no need to bother one of the doctors'.

Now she opens her soft mouth.
'You've got no substance, George;
you're like that cake.'

QUEEN SACRIFICE

There are games they play to ritualize their griefs.
They involve the giving and receiving of pain . . .

For their anniversary her mother
gives them the furled buds of a lily,
a painted plate to furnish symbols.
They have closed the years
of silk and lace, those subtle drifts
and slips, the pale milk of them.
Now, reaching fourteen years,
they harden to ivory. She moves.

1. P−K4, P−K4; 2. P−KN3, P−KN3;
3. B−N2, B−N2; 4. N−K2, N−K2;

Light and shade. Light strokes
the symmetry of the board,
her nails' polish. The squares
lead off into Dutch interiors,
those swaddled women, their heads
bound − immaculately − in linen,
a dream of the sea's puckered surface,
and the restless pieces settling
into unaccustomed places.

5. P−Q3, QN−B3; 6. 0−0, 0−0;
7. P−KB4, P×P; 8. B×P . . .

He smiles, at what he would call
'her remarkable sacrifice'. Inside her,
the embryo floats, little fish,
pleading for its existence . . .
saying 'give it up, give it up'
of everything but itself.
She, though, would have these pieces

coloured like blood; the figures alive,
their eyes glittering with a wink
of evil. She will not look at him.

. . . B×P; 9. N−Q2, B×R; 10. Q×B . . .

'The queen exerts enormous pressure
on the long diagonal.' His smile wavers.

. . . P−B3; 11. B−R6, R−B2; 12. R×P, Q−K1;
13. N−KB3, R×R; 14. Q×R, Q−B2; 15. Q−B3, P−Q4;
16. N−N5, P−Q5; 17. N×QP, Q−B3;

And she knows he will have her
held and cast; sand will drift over her;
she will whiten into rage and silence;
she will be a Dutch girl, plaited,
strangled. She would not make a sound.

18. N×N − 'the rebellion of the pinned piece' − ,
Q×Q; 19. N×Nch, K−R1; 20. N−B7 checkmate.

Orange petals peel to the clamour
of a blotched throat, calling her
from the voices of children
to the triumph of a hollow victory.
'Had Black chosen the right moment
the game might have been saved . . .
this is loss by queen sacrifice.'

STOCKTAKING

Today, the sky is heaped above
a rudimentary smudge of puddled fens;
along the dyke, the water is ridged and olive.
The wind turns it over and over.
He is carrying his pain carefully – a reliquary,
or something brimming, which he must not spill.

The tractors are awash, axle-deep
in a green, school-knicker sea of brassicas
and, against the sky, the long-barrow clamps
are ossuaries for yellow mangolds.
Out on the chequerboard fields a straggle of sheep
mumble the sprout stalks, like obedient poodles.
Their bellies are lamb-fat.

All around him his farm is laid out,
a spreadsheet, an itinerary of routines.
Yet all he can see is the careful doctor,
pulling the screens around those text-book eyes,
and telling him in a prescriptive tone
of lambs that he'll not fatten,
of glistening kingcups
whose drowned heads he'll never see.

MORPHOLOGY

A murderer drifts. Park leaves waste
themselves against the railings, wait,
like he does, for one of the white-
faced girls to disappear in wet
darkness, under the laurels. What
hushed attention stirs the leaves and him!

Next. There is a tip-tap of sole
and heel, stalked darkly through the stale
puddles of streetlights where the spill
and scent of midnight gathers. He'll spoil
her pretty daydreams, relish her shrilled
fear. He loves the lives of these thin women!

While this one kills with a kiss.
He smothers the pincers of her case-
notes, covers her face, as she chose,
as she chose. Weeps while his pleas cross
with her to silence. And those claws,
unhooking slowly from her skin.

How does this man tell of the drill
of her crying and how he would 'deal
with it'? And though his baby doll
is broken, he never meant . . . ? He drools,
his fingers tremble in the dial.
'It was like a red mist, closing in . . . '

So, unfocussed as their victims,
they have as little in common
as any strangers; only their dreams.
And tomorrow's murderers? Turn them
as you will, you'll find them clean
as bones, waiting for conjunction.

CENTURY

I THE MATRIARCH

So leather-hearted, springing back like saplings
growing round her gate her sons were twined
around her will, bark-hardened to her orders.
After they changed from frightened boys to men
she squatted in the bedroom with a darkened face
and called out names of sepia ghosts. 'Mother?'
And put on smiles in pinafores to quaver
'Is it you?' She knew the walls would whisper
secrets if she screwed her eyes up tight;
routes and destinations through the stars.

'She's getting old': they touched their temples.
'Please be kind.' And yet – she'd stared
so hard into the mirror's fly-marked promises.
When dark cars brought them back from church
each one sat in silence; trying not to hear
the rustling walls while sticky sherry cloyed
their tongues. Then moved around the house,
hanging sheets across the emptied looking-glass,
drawing the curtains tight, tight. Against
the pin-holes sprinkled on a shuttered sky.

II THE MINER

The wheel spins – such precise geometry
as dark shutters close against the sky.
Shafts core the hillsides; clean burrows
for the coal-faced men whose hearts grow dust.

Each day turns its back on the blown rows
stuffed like a greengrocer's. Four faces
watch him go, bright pennies paid for buckets
where the caterpillars land in clotted heaps.

In their dreams he is always falling, falling
away from them. Yet when they go to Brid
he knots his handkerchief from ear to ear,
then shows surprising legs like pallid roots,

and tunnels for their smiles. But soon
his bike is clocking on and off again.
One day the youngest son will grow
to count the molehills forming on his lawn.

As his sister tells him something inexplicable
– of a lift-shaft to the sky, where their father's
coal-blue face waits to stretch into a smile –
he'll see nothing but that blinded tunnelling.

III THE CANAL WALK

Such sharp edges, someone has cut them.
So brimming full, and the sword reflections.

A child's face hangs in the ripples:
hello, hello. Leeches loop here

and the newts are sieving water
through their little hands, their feet.

This is a swing bridge. Which springs
beneath her feet and then dissolves

in presences and absences for prehistory
of barges, nudging on between the locks.

In March, catkins wave their tails and
pussy willows purr under her fingers;

the reservoir is a grass wall. Up there
sails and swans move against the sky.

Now the canal rips itself in two. Goodbye.
And one half slides around the corner.

A big 'O' bounces on the surface. Bricks drip.
The twinned canoe slips in and disappears.

Mummy, Daddy, keep me safe. Do not let me fall.
The water makes a noise, like swallowing.

IV THE FARMER

Look for me in weeds at the churchyard wall.
Where at my feet the land fumbles down the valley,
and at my head the grit cliff frowns. Easter brings
a trinity of crosses bristling on the sky, like thorns.

This is a cold bed, trenched and narrow;
I jostle for my headroom, rocks ringing on the spade.
My children eat the harvest of green stubble
and in it taste the stones that made their bread.

Talk to me of roots. Here are mine grown down and up
and through the emptied spaces of my eyes. Yet I see
my farm is still three-cornered, its thinning pastures
patched to an eiderdown of stone fields on the hill.

From the water meadows, it's just a smudge against
a blown sky, an interruption in the trees
where hard-mouthed sheep mumble on its grass.
My son is a bent figure, hooked to his spade.

The seasons roll like millstones. Yet every spring
brings rock-roses resurrected from the soil.
Look for me in weeds at the churchyard wall. These are
my roots; my canopy is stretched across the clouds.

V THE CHILDREN

Where trolls omit to squat and wait
the corkscrew path makes crooked
invitations. This way, children.
Bracken waves dark arms, dark spores.
These mountains wear quiet wraps;
when their scarves are gone
the bones show through. Blank faces
stare across the valley's chisel.
The air shivers. Water over rocks,
and such new voices, splintering.

A piebald chain, of trees, no trees.
High summer grazing, fir-coated, gone,
and the bald hill opposite yawns
with one dead mouth. Slate-works
metamorphosed into relics, blue pallor.
While at the summit, now, the children
stand above the tree-line looking past
the crazy faces of the hills. And on
towards an unobstructed 'v'. Where
all that water meets and joins the sky.

Patricia Doubell

THE FARCE

Last night I dreamed of my lover, who I kissed,
A blind and ecstatic odyssey of a kiss,
But at the end I opened my eyes on a stranger,
Armed with the boredom of all things exotic.
How we both laughed!

And in the chaos of my lover's room –
Books, bottles, saucepans, violins, knives, and rings –
A squirrel played – hiding and finding its winter stores –
Marked by a fatal disease
Well known among squirrels.

We slept, four in a bed, my lover and I,
The stranger, and a famous opera singer,
Tipping the scale at a generous fifteen stone,
The squirrel interred us under the snow of sheets.
How we all laughed!

What happened there, I cannot, now, remember,
Or will not,
Or dare not,
Perhaps neither dream or nightmare,
But how we laughed!

MAZURKA NO 2

Beryl has dragged her boyfriend to the ballet,
There should be common interests – after all
There's more to life than sex and revolution.
Prelude and valse – already his boots are restless,
The true mazurka fidgeting under the leather.

from LINES FROM A LARGE OFFICE

There was a young woman from Combe
Who had suffered a scrape of the womb,
She was quickly surrounded
By those who abounded
With similar stories in Combe.

A nasty old man from Gleneagles
Was tormented by bloodhounds and beagles,
When they asked 'Why so grim?'
He said *they* pursued *him*,
Which was why he threw stones at the seagulls.

A lively young lady called Molly
Wore tights and a star-spangled brolly,
But a sensible aunt
Told her 'Molly! You can't!
You should never wear tights with a brolly.'

There was an old man from Redruth
Who was wary of telling the truth,
On account of its size
One should mix it with lies,
Said that wily old man from Redruth.

There was a young girl from Fermanagh
Who had bought a bassoon and a banner,
They kept her content,
For wherever she went,
She was cheered in a ponderous manner.

There lived an old man in a kennel
On a diet of hogwash and fennel,
It was not for his crimes
Or for writing rude rhymes,
But he would have his own private kennel.

There was a young lady of Woking
Who made a large bear give up smoking,
When they said 'Watch his claws!'
She beguiled it with gauze
And assumed that her friends must joking.

There was an old man with a flute
Who could never afford a new suit,
So, dressed in large bags,
Notwithstanding the snags,
he pursued his amours with his flute.

An earnest young man from the Hook
Gave an angry gorilla a book,
It chewed up the chairs,
Threw him headfirst downstairs,
And astutely dismembered that book.

A charming young girl from the Rhine
Was too large at the base of the spine,
But in Naples and Rome
Where she soon made her home,
They considered this failing divine.

THE DANCING VICAR

Jerk up the curtain,
The footlights flicker,
The spotlight lands on the dancing vicar,
Bundle of energy, fervour, and charm,
Shot of new blood in a half-dead arm,
Only mammon can mend the roof,
Beat it up, Vicar,
Cleave that hoof!

Why should a man
With the vaudeville feet
Choose to perform at the Sunday-school treat?
Now worldly gain couldn't be the clue,
For a dancing bishop would hardly do,
Can a soul be saved by the jazz-man's beat?
I doubt it, Vicar,
But – dig that heat!

The clerics cant-compromise,
Bargain and bungle,
The Ladies' Guild is the usual jungle,
The inner music seems mute or drowned
In the super-sonorganized merry-go-round.
But the roof must be mended with hotcha-chas,
Or the congregation might see the stars.

What is it sifts out of the dead-pan pelf?
Why, the shining ascent of the vicar himself,
In the midst of it all there's a hope grown faint;
Yes, it might add up if it bred a saint.
The spot-light's lost him, the drums beat quicker,
Go it you jazz-men!
Come on, Vicar!

THE RUNAWAY HEART

Did you hear the story of Boss McGroo?
He was awful sick and they said he was through,
Then along came the men of the medical art,
And they fixed him up with a plastic heart
Up and down up and down up and down –

And that old ticker was a stayer and a sticker,
With a dogged old din like Rin-tin-tin,
With a postulating clangour of a spanner in the works,
It was givin' him the jiggers and the jeebees and the jerks,
It was givin' him insomnia day and night,
He could turn him left, he could turn him right,
Now ho down death for a sting-a-ling-ling,
But 'twas 'gainst the law to stop the thing
Up and down up and down up and down –

Now McGroo was a man never tangled with the law,
The millions that he made were always making plenty more,
Well, some said five and some said seven,
But he'd made that money with good clean livin',
He bowed him low to the bald-headed eagle,
And his word to the young men was 'Do it legal.'
Up and down up and down up and down –

But he knowed of a man in Arkansaw,
He'd had some dealin's with him before,
He'd had occasion to use his gun,
Paid him well for a job well done,
That man could shoot like he'd give you a pill,
And the name of that man was Billy the Kill,
So he went to that man, and said 'Billy be smart,
Put a bullet right through this goddam heart.'
'But Boss, you're crazy,' Billy replied,
'I got my principles, got my pride,
An' I never shot at a crazy man,
There's things you can't do, an' things you can,

I never shot a man that wanted to die,
And you didn't oughta ask that much of a guy.'
Up and down up and down up and down –

Then McGroo said Billy was mean and cheap,
And he called him chicken and a pimp and a creep,
And he cussed him up into one big heap,
And he wouldn't let him eat, and he wouldn't let him sleep,
Last thing he said he'd double the figure,
And Billy began to debate with his trigger,
And he sure was havin' some rough ride,
Overcomin' his principles and his pride
Up and down up and down up and down –
He put his hand in his pocket at last,
And he heaved a sigh, he didn't draw fast,
But the gun in his hand shone black and glossy,
When in walked the sheriff with a six man posse
Up and down up and down up and down –

'You kin shoot that man in Mexico
Or any place else you care to go,
You gotta live, you gotta kill,
I don't condone it, but I guess you will,
You kin bury 'em deep under six foot o' turf,
But not in a town where I'm the shurf.'
Up and down up and down up and down –

Then McGroo lit out with one big yell,
And what he did then would be hard to tell,
For the hammer of the heart-beat rose and fell
Like a hammer on the clamour of the damned in Hell,
And he hit the roof, and he shook the ground,
And he laughed and he hollered, and he danced around,
And he frit the life out of Billy and the boys,
'Twas the only way he could drown the noise,
And the runaway heart went over the hill,
McGroo! McGroo!
And the runaway heart went over the hill,
And for all I know she's going still,

Up and down up and down, and the prairie tells
Of a millionaire said his fare ye wells
To the heart-beat hammering of Hell's own bells
Up and down up and down up and down up and down
Up and down up and down up and down –

THE DEGRADATION
OF JEHOSHOPHAT SNUDGE

My friends, listen well
To this tale I shall tell,
And it's better to pity than judge,
How an unspotted cowboy to ruin was lured,
Then weep for Jehoshophat Snudge.

Now Jehosh never gambled
Nor spat on the floor,
And no girl did he take to his bed,
And iffan his horse took a shine to a mare
He would hit the poor thing on the head.

The taste of rye whisky
Had ne'er passed his lips,
His ten gallon hat was pure white,
Till a man in a black hat, with evil designs,
Made Jehosh give up doing things right.

In a sinful saloon,
Which was called Rising Moon,
They enticed him to play games of chance,
Then they heartlessly gave him rye whisky to drink,
While the girls did an evil French dance.

And those girls kept him in,
Doing all kinds of sin,
Through the door they would not let him pass
Until he was knackered, and broke, and blind drunk,
Then they threw him outside on the grass.

As he lay in the gutter,
Unable to utter
The words that was burnin' inside him,
A hog, which had wandered a bit off its beat
Came over and lay down beside him.

He wouldn't have cared
But that hog must have heard
What a girl passing by chanced to say:
'You must judge ev'ry creep by the comp'ny he'll keep.'
And that hog wandered slowly away.

Oh! There's many a man
Will do wrong if he can,
And maybe there's one here tonight;
Remember the name of Jehoshophat Snudge,
And just you keep on doing right.

THE OPERA HOUSE

*A young Irishman who has worked on the building
of Sydney Opera House writes home to his sweetheart.*

O Mary, my Mary, the contract is ended,
With Seamus, your brother, I'm now out of work,
But while we had breath t'was Himself we defended,
And now we shall rest in the county of Cork.

For myself and young Seamus have winged o'er the ocean,
And landed long since in this fair land of wealth,
Where lies, like a swan that's come down in slow motion,
The opera house that was built by Himself.

And Himself was the one that we pinned our hopes high on,
The flow of his cloak, and the mane of his hair –
The sweep of his arm was the sword of King Bryan,
His eye was a hawk as it hangs in the air.

And didn't the Lord Mayor come poking and prying,
Our time was too long for his hopes and his fears,
And who but Himself said 'Be done with your crying,
For Westminster Abbey took five hundred years.'

So I said to Seamus 'I'm sending for Mary,
For five hundred years is a lifetime for sure,
I'll keep her in comfort, she'll live like a fairy,
And still we'll have money for Guinness galore.'

But came a false woman with eyes like an owlet's,
And who should be showing her round but Himself,
And all she'd be saying was 'Where are the toilets?' –
'And where is the plumbing to safeguard our health?'

Myself and young Seamus made venture to say
She had mentioned a thing that was five blocks away,
And if that was too far, there were houses around,
And good-natured folk in the world to be found,
And anyone seeing a lady in trouble
Would ask her inside, and she'd gladly pay double.

We showed her the place where the great would be dining,
Red velvet and crystal, a sight for the eye,
Soft lights on fine linen and silver were shining,
'But where are the kitchens?' she said with a sigh.

Then I looked at Seamus and Seamus at me,
For we had a small kettle for brewing the tea,
And the quality mostly have meat on their shelves,
And would greatly prefer what they'd cook for themselves,
They would have the idea they were getting it free
If they brought in their dinner like Seamus and me.

But she wouldn't be still, it was no good explaining,
The holes in the roof were for seeing the stars,
And it wasn't Himself who could stop it from raining –
She said 'Where's the space for the parking of cars?'

She brought the Town Council down, squawking and clacking,
Himself answered then with the pride of a prince,
And he said it was bodies and souls they were lacking,
Then torned on his hale, and we've not seen him since.

And a terrible beauty has gone from the world,
And a flag is torn down that was bravely unfurled,
There are some would be pushing the great to the wall
With their toilets and kitchens and car parks and all,
And the termites take over the glory of kings
Who would never have bothered their heads with such things.
There are Cromwells all over that pillage and rob,
Putting good honest bricklayers out of a job.

CLOWN IN A BURST OF GENEROSITY

Clown, in a burst of generosity,
Made a present of all his possessions –
Masks, motley, hat, coat, trousers, vest, underpants, shrugs,
    sighs, sausages, and a multitude of disguises –
To his lovers, and how they laughed,
Kicking the glad rags into the winds of change.

Mimi Khalvati

EVERGREEN

It was past green fields and pines
the Jews were cattled and the last thing
her witch's eyes could see – thirteen
million pairs they say – was the green
of the hill turning away like a mother
turning to take her children home.

And I have lived with green in playing-fields,
neighbours' gardens seeping poison
through the fence: ground-elder flaunting
height and health where colour should have been,
the colours of my childhood, needed more than ever
in a land that has adopted me, that turns me grey;

while the dress my mother danced in, golden
polka-dots and flounces, circles on its own,
sad as old-time vaudeville, and camel, camel-
lilac of the slopes where shepherds' lives
meet poppy every day, has settled on the leaves
of war, and every leaf has turned.

Even blues are not the same: of tiles,
of domes, of skies too dazed for blue;
or of shadows, mulberry-blue, in the room
you enter blinded, learning how to see again
gloom becoming someone dear, a grandmother
who gives you grapes she has quietly washed.

And white, like all the colours of the world
raising home, hazy as the verandahs
you half-remember, is something to avoid
in a land where no one's hands are clean;
where dust is never sand but more a mirage
no one even yearns for, intent on lawns.

FAMILY FOOTNOTES

My arms in the sink, I half-listen
as someone keeps me company:
she's such a sweetiepie, isn't she?
I pause and to my own surprise

realize, seeing her suddenly through the eyes
of guests how small she seems;
like a robin redbreast perched with other
mothers I thank god aren't mine.

My father cracks a joke on the transatlantic
line, misreading my alliances;
decades of regret still failing
to make her an easy butt.

But his laugh is warm bubble, a devil
to slip into, like the fold of his cheek
and the film of his eye, film that I know
my own before long will look through.

My children are with me, as always, my son
even now sleeping under covers
I have no more to do with. He is always
loving. To say this, to think this

seems suspect in a world such as ours.
How have we escaped it?
My daughter is about to bumble in the door,
late as usual, and be sweet to me,

nattering on as I clatter in the kitchen,
her breasts within an inch of my arm.
Nothing seems to rattle her: embarrassments
that floor me, still, at my age.

She is chock-a-block with courage;
fresh air on her cheeks like warpaint.
Pooled in this – this love – and this – and this –
what has riddled me to long for more?

WOMAN, STONE AND BOOK

And I woke one night
in tears from a terrible dream
of a small stone house
with a central chimney, a spiral
staircase and grapes on the window-sill.
I later learnt: *you are describing*
a peasant cottage of the sixteenth century
to be found all over Europe – France,
Poland, Germany. That puts a different
slant on it. The hologram again
adjusting angles of vision receding
into history asserting the right
to unfold itself, perhaps being
itself a section, a skin some godly
presence is peering in to learn
something of what it is to be human.

And I woke one night
in tears from a terrible dream
of a small stone house
and I said to the old woman writer
beside me *I've been here before.*
For some strange reason
the woman's name was Katharine.
Katharine? What does Katharine
mean to you? Katharine Mansfield
was the only name that came to me.

I lived in a house called Mansfield Place,
a small brick cottage in peachy pink
where my children were raised,
a spiral staircase painted blue
holding faces adjusting angles
to my line of vision. I was the big one
in those years. From the turn of the stair
that one about Tom when he was little:
Tom fly he yelled and he flew,
landing on my back in the hall
bending to pick up wellingtons.
Accidents of life preserving it?
Or patterns' interferences, mute
as the backs of angels who break men's fall?

And I had been there before in dreams
playing games of hide and seek
through currant bushes and neighbours'
gardens forgetting now what I was
searching for if I knew it then.
Something to do with infidelity
I think. In those years these were
things we suffered from with our hands
in each others' pockets striving
to become one skin. Letting go,
struggling now to fill our own.

And I asked myself
why are you crying and answered
I am forty-three and have understood
in a dream of woman stone and book
what all those people mean
and why they mourn
and how clean I have been
through all those years of innocence.

I take a coffee break and pick up
threads going every which way knowing
it can't matter much which thread
I choose to follow, homing as they do
to junctions; conditions infinite
as connections, our mothers' whispers.

Two camps. The lover and the beloved.
The innocent and the betrayed. Meaning
that to move out of the oppressor's camp
is to forfeit innocence. Meaning
that to catch oneself at the point
of crossing a line is to wake in tears.

There is the fence. There is the wood.
There is the hunter by his billboard
for trespassers. Here is my face.
Scents of trails criss-cross the undergrowth
dense as twigs. A bird's hopping is enough
to turn tail for, only to come out at night
sniffing the air clean, criss-crossed by moons
and witches' brooms and cries of women
pricking the wood's seven layers of skin:
drops of berries beading a trail
of witness, where the enemy has been.

A *POST-FEMINIST* DAWN

There are dawns of stone and pit: dead ends
whichever way you turn. A lover's note. Friends
who run in grooves our mouths should have sucked
rooting for the teat of depressions they have licked
hungry for the milk, the empathy to spurt from it.

We who live in limbo
fungus, fern and fallacy
We who lie in utero
waste-products of phallocracy
We who dream of dawns

submit: crazed with the flog of directives
crumpling our anger like cupid's missives
under pillows to corrupt our dreams, to make us
doubt the dawns our sisters wake to, out of focus
on a shore we cannot swim to in our reluctance to admit

the dream, the light, the ocean
how much has failed to fit
the picture painted for us children
the picture as We painted it
We who were framed.

And I ask myself, I ask you, is this it? All
that we were raised for, groped for, from the first bawl
at our mother's thigh, to the last clambering in?
No, there is more, you would answer, thinking in
terms you would hate me to think of as *making it*.

What are We to make of it?
We who are womb and foetus?
We who see both sides of it?
Must we swing, celibate, in the hiatus
of the dusk, till mother calls us in?

Or, loving women, have a better time of it? Invulnerable,
penetrable, in an age that breeds without us, the reversal
of what it means to have power or be powerless, to have blood
without a wound, to have seed with a consequence, to have food
for mouths not our own; even now, in the thick of it

fixed by those who frame us
spayed by a fear stronger
than the impetus to love and to fail us
canker We are not; and larger
than the dawn's small stash of it.

STONE OF PATIENCE

In the old days, she explained to a grandchild bred in England,
in the old days in Persia, it was the custom to have a stone,
a special stone you would choose from a rosebed, or a goat-patch,
a stone of your own to talk to, tell your troubles to,
a stone we called, as they now call me, a stone of patience.

No therapists then to field a question with another,
but stones from dust where ladies' fingers, cucumbers
basked in sun. Were the ones they used for gherkins
babies that would have grown, like piano tunes had we known
the bass beyond the first few bars? Or miniatures?

Some things I'm content to guess: colour in a calyx-tip,
is it gold or mauve? A girl or a boy . . . Patience
was so simple then: waiting for the clematis to open,
to purple on a wall; the bud to shoot out stamens,
the jet of milk to leave its rim like honey

on the bee's fur. But patience when the cave is sealed,
a boulder at the door, is riled by the scent of hyacinth
in the blue behind the stone: the willow by the pool
where once she sat to trim a beard with kitchen scissors,
to tilt her hat at smiles, at sleep, at congratulations.

And a woman, faced with a lover grabbing for his shoes
when women-friends would have put themselves in hers,
no longer knows what's virtuous. Will anger shift
the boulder, buy her freedom, and the earth's? Or patience,
like the earth's, be abused? Even nonchalance

can lead to courage, to conception: a voice that says
oh come on darling, it'll be alright, oh do let's.
How many children were born from words such as these?
I know my own were; now learning to repeat them, to outgrow
a mother's awe of consequences her body bears.

So now that midsummer, changing shape, has brought in
another season, the grape becoming raisin, hinting
in a nip at the sweetness of a clutch, one fast upon another;
now that the breeze is raising sighs from sheets
as she tries to learn again, this time for herself,

to fling caution to the winds like colour in a woman's skirt
or to borrow patience from the stones in her own backyard
where fruit still hangs on someone else's branch . . . don't ask her
whose? as if it mattered. Say: *they won't mind*
as you reach for a leaf, for the branch, and pull it down.

SEVENSES

At seven, skirting a verandah, pausing to seduce
an arabesque from heaven down to a pirouette, I entrance
the lovers from their leaning shapes under the shade
of scaffolding to applaud for encores whose echoes on an island
describe my cause in cups inscribed with my difficult
name. I dance to its tune, newly pronounced.

At forty-two, meeting a man of forty-nine,
turning the land on a dig to find slivers of time
to patch the potter's clay, I treasure what is found,
what is mine, glance at the vessels on the ground, my ware;
failing to define the chalice in the air, I resign myself
to the figures' stoop in rings within rings of the dance.

RICE

i

Ten years later, I recognize his profile in a Tehran cab.
You see these teeth, he said, leaning across the passengers,
what became of me? . . . I see him silhouetted in dazzle
as the tunnel ends on the last lap to Frankfurt, his hand
on the window's metal lip, his cap in the other circling
like a bird then, loosed on the wind, beating a tattoo

against the wires as I watch him reach to the rack for his case,
send that too struggling through the window, socks and all.
I have come, he declared, *to start at the start* . . . Now, a decade
later, he asks: *You see these teeth?* He bares them in the light
to show how short, how straight they are. *What became of me:
you wonder why?* His fist emerges from his pocket, clenched.

*I eat it all the time. My hand is never still, like a swallow
at its nest, going in, going out. Not a grain escapes.*
He fingers his moustache. *I even check in wing-mirrors.
See how it's worn my teeth right down?* His hand unfurls,
dabs at the proffered air between us. *Please, have some.*
What, raw? I ask. *It's rice,* he urges. *Rice.*

ii

I have fled on mules, the star of Turkey in my sky, to start
at the start. I have come like sleet with Mary in the dark; swum
into hedgerows by the line. Gifts of weave and leather tucked
in polythene for friends, already fled or free, are dry.
Will they harbour us, we wonder, ten years, a revolution later,
towel us from swollen rivers chanting MARG BAR ÉMRIKÁ*?

* *Death to America*

iii

The cabs still carry passengers: my mother in her black chador,
my sisters among soldiers, now and them a face blasted
like a cake. They have granted me asylum. I write plays.
A friend I love in London has hung the Kurdish mules
I brought her on the same hook as an old sitar she never
plays. When she dusts them she thinks of me, and of rivers.

I told her of the man I met twice: once in a train,
once again in Tehran in those early days . . . what days they
      were . . .
Ah well. Her sister lives near Washington; the husband –
      an Iranian –
works for the Department of Defence, and in real estate;
      comes home
to scan *The Post*, its leaders on Japan: po-faced as she snatches
victory from jaws set ever closer as they wing towards Potomac.

CHILDREN OF HIROSHIMA

On a good-girl Sunday afternoon
walking with my mother in Regent's Park,
linking arms like signoras and signorinas
in piazzas we have visited, we talk a language
of our own, happy to be overheard, free
to be personal in level voices mingling
Farsi with Latin and the smell of roses.

A royal occasion and she a slip of a girl
honoured by an invitation to be one of the maidens
who bring in the trays for the bride, heaped
with petals from the rainbow on the peacock lawn,
their names as strange as Woburn Abbey,
Centifolia Bullata and Paddy McGredy –
is a story I have already half-forgotten.

I see the yellow roses where we stood.
Each bed was perfect, each favourite superseded
until our backs began to ache and we headed
for the car, our separate lives forking
like the path by the gate, leaving stoic
heathers together with old-age pensioners
to mind the cold, colder in the grate.

One bed alone was trampled. Near the gate.
Just as we were leaving. Just one bed.
As though a heavy weight had come down on it,
from nowhere. Long-stemmed pink roses
clustered in rings like bridesmaids' wreaths
were pressing to the ground as though a boot,
a giant boot, was holding down their heads;

as though they alone had been singled out
to bear the brunt of hurricanes, some mean
revenge, some poison rising from the soil
to sap the strength their neighbours had,
so pristine in their regiments, to resist
whatever scourge laid low down this bed.
From above or below? I looked for signs.

There was only one: CHILDREN OF HIROSHIMA.
Children of Hiroshima? It doesn't make sense.
So some breeder allows his conscience to play
name-games with small pink roses . . .
but what has happened to the bed? Why this bed?
When my children are sick I hide it from my mother.
But now I need her eyes, her wonder. I show her.

Children of Hiroshima. She pronounces it differently.
She is shocked. My shock seems greater than hers.
I whip her up. She is moved to tears. Are they real?
I protect the roses. I wish I hadn't told her.
She keeps on talking. I keep on talking.
We exchange analyses; handicapped by horticultural
foolishness, and Farsi. We turn to English.

Patting herself, her hand ungloved, as though someone
had stolen her wealth, my mother says:
I shall never forget this as long as I live.
And I feel like the child she kept on telling:
*I live only for you, if it weren't for you,
my darling* . . . as sceptical, as guilty, as lonely
as the child who vowed to live only for herself.

EARLS COURT

I brush my teeth harder when the gum bleeds.
Arrive alone at parties, leaving early.

The tide comes in, dragging the stare
of my eyes from pastures I could call my own.

Through the scratches on the record – '*Ah! Vieni, vieni!*'* –
I concentrate on loving.

I use my key. No duplicate of this.
Arrive alone at parties, leaving early.

I brush my teeth harder when the gum bleeds.
Sing to the fern in the steam. Not even looking:

commuters buying oranges, Italian vegetables,
bucket flowers from shores I might have danced in, briefly.

I use my key: a lost belonging on the stair.
Sing to the fern in the steam. I wash my hair.

The tide goes out, goes out. The body's wear and tear.
Commuters' faces turn towards me: bucket flowers.

A man sits eyeing destinations on the train.
He wears Islamic stubble, expensive clothes, two rings.

He talks to himself in Farsi, loudly like a drunk.
Laughs aloud to think where life has brought him.

Eyeing destinations on the train – a lost belonging –
talks to himself with a laugh I could call my own.

* *from Puccini's* Madam Butterfly

Like a drunk I want to neighbour him; sit beside
his stubble's scratch; turn his talking into chatting.

I want to tell him I have a ring like his,
only smaller. I want to see him use his key.

I want to hear the child who runs to him call
Baba! I want to hear him answer, turning

from his hanging coat: *Beeya, Babajune, beeya!*
'*Ah! Vieni, vieni . . .* '

'THE POPPY SIGNALS TIME
TO SCYTHE THE WHEAT'

I quote my mother though I don't suppose
she scanned it quite like that but found a brief
and simpler way to say that poppy grows
when wheat is ripe, like anger, love or grief.
For anger cannot foster change when dumb
to fault a man, nor love that cannot scythe
his pride fulfil him; grief will not succumb
to guilt that bears a grudge to bear a wreath.
No anger, love or grief will harvest good
till men can learn to listen, women learn
to speak, and turn their dreams to likelihood
of change and peace, redress and union.
    The day he died my mother cried all night,
    her tendrils round me, wound towards the light.

Felicity Napier

BLINIS

Tonight, as I prepared them
Puffed, small and dappled brown
As they should have been,
I thought of Baboushka
In the long Parisian afternoons
Flattening the bubbles of flour
With a worn wooden spoon and stirring,
Stirring the honey-coloured cream.
I was allowed to whip the egg whites dry
and paint a swirl of butter in the pan.
I don't remember eating them
Just the stooped, content, old lady
So engrossed and certain of her art.
Later, she would take me through
The spotted curling photographs
That lined her walls with comfort
And bring me to her other life –
A sepia land of country dachas, carriages
And wooden colonels taking tea.
We journeyed far from the damp, small flat,
With the ikons by the door, on the right,
The dust-woven rugs from Algeria
And the little blackened blinis pan.

Baboushka, my life is fast and easy now;
I do not use your old and slow techniques,
But should it change as yours did
And leave me unprepared,
Please pray for me,
For I've lost my Bible and my wooden spoon.

NATASHA SAYS

She was a fellow vegetarian and Friend of the Earth,
who went to his Tuesday yoga class.
She looked like Janey Morris
and of course he fell in love with her.
He called her Goddess and begged her to live with him.

Within a month he knew he'd made a bad mistake:
she was too submissive, too tearful;
he wanted a woman who'd be an equal,
as well as beautiful and feminine,
a vegetarian and Friend of the Earth.

'I'm going to France for a couple of weeks'
he announced, 'you must be gone by my return.'
'Yes Robert' she sighed, dabbing at her eyes.
He kissed her briefly on the cheek;
she waved him goodbye and set to work.

First, she took his jug and watered the pillows,
the duvet, the sofa, the red velvet curtains,
the matting in the hall and his fine kelim.
Like Demeter, she scattered the small black seeds,
humming to herself, and sprinkling more water.

Then she dialled; listened to the New York Speaking Clock
and gently laid the receiver on the duvet;
it would lie, like a slug, awaiting the growth
of the bright sprigged pile of mustard and cress –
so good for you – and she slammed his door.

RETREAT

I met him in a restaurant near the Madeleine
and while we waited for his wife to come
his fingers galloped on his chair.
Twice during lunch he took out his pen
to draw up maps on the paper cloth.

He'd been that morning to the Faubourg St Honoré
to a shop selling uniforms and tin toy soldiers
then afterwards to see Napoleon's tomb.
He'd looked in the military sections of bookshops,
and bought a book about the Occupation of Paris.

At two o'clock he put on his coat, fastened
the little leather grenades and barked goodbye.
His boots resounded on the cobbles like gunshot.
And tacking along behind, with packages in her arms,
went his wife, a potential deserter.

APPLE TIME

He is going to bed in the square red building.
Around him are fields and four more hospitals.
He undresses, draws the curtains round his cot
and takes the pills they have given him.
'Yes' they say 'your doctor will come next week.'

In their house, alight with books and pictures,
a red setter, a bird, fish and the new hamster,
the children have taken themselves to bed.
She sits on in the kitchen amongst the litter
of his departure. The receiver is off the hook.

At breakfast he chooses sausages, as before,
signs himself up for an hour of creative therapy
and isolates his ten p. pieces for the phone.
'Bring the typewriter, I'll have another go –
and I need a padlock for my cupboard door.'

Chin on hands, she is a triangle of hopelessness;
two china tea-leaves cross like swords in her cup.
It's happened again. She sees him spot-lit in the hall
last night. She kisses his cheek goodbye,
his knuckles grip white on their weekend case.

By four o'clock he is in the visitors' room,
in front of children's television. She should be here.
His mind is thick and light like foam. He doesn't care.
She arrives with chocolate cake and books, the kids,
a padlock and a typewriter. He cannot speak to her.

'Look at all the apples, children. Nurse said
you could go and pick some to take home with us.'
Turning from the screen they file out silently.
The parents watch them cartwheel on the empty lawn.
'I'll make an apple pie for you.' He does not smile.

After them the door is slammed. She hears the easy click
of a lock and the rattle of keys on a belt.
At the window his hand is raised like the Buddha's,
calling the earth to witness. The children bicker
in the car; in front of her is distance and a grey road.

HANDYMAN

He had the cheek – grotesquely pink
and stinking of cologne – to rise up
in her dream. He was typing at her desk
and paused to wave a pudgy hand . . .
'Sweet lady, Hello. Make yourself at home.

I've nearly finished. Today just roses,
and peppers. Next time the strudel
and garlic sausage.' She finds a home
for six green peppers, pneumatic and shiny;
but she doesn't even like them.

Her hammer descends on the rose stems.
If only, she thinks, the fat pink worms
of his fingers would STOP. On her bed
reclines his rat-grey leather jacket . . .
she adds a body and massive, thrusting thighs . . .

The back of his neck and his torso
are matted with curling ginger hair.
'Look here, Mr Titovitch, I'm sorry,
I don't need you today, I really don't.
The waste disposal hasn't jammed,

the heating's OK and the hoover . . . '
Ting, ting, goes the typewriter carriage.
'One moment, dear lady, one moment.'
He stands, unzips the paper, clicks
his Serbo-Croat heels. Great moons

of sweat have risen in his armpits.
The glossy brow beneath his crew-cut
weeps on his belly's protrusion. Imagine,
she thinks, imagine sex with THAT!
How dare he arrive unannounced like this –

how dare he compromise me? I won't
stand for it. I won't, I WILL NOT.
'Now my favourite lady, listen to me.'
With a little bow he reads out the account.
'1. For the willing acceptance of all flowers,

chocolates, pastries and delicatessen goods,
including smoked ham, for seven years . . .
2. For permitting me, in smart clothes,
to clean your lavatory, unblock your drains
and tend your ageing stove without payment.

3. For calling me out at night to change tyres.
4. For loan of my van in March last year,
and for accepting lunch that day at Garibaldi's.
5. For foiling my attempts to kiss you
or embrace you, with weakening resolve, and

6. For making me fall in love with you . . .
All this, dear lady, will cost you more
than the price of salami: your false innocence,
no less'. 'Oh Tito, Tito, no!' she screams . . .
but reader, he had his wicked way with her.

NO SOUVENIRS

A winter and spring have gone
and still I don't believe it.
Going back to the village I see you
in a car or walking up the street.
I hear your voice and wheel around
in the baker's shop. My heart stops
at your open bedroom window,
the newly planted pansies by your door.

Does your husband smooth the ripples now
in the dusty pink bedspread I sent from abroad,
or do its creases deepen in the cupboard
where your stiff clothes hang?
I remember the dandelion coffee;
with the dog as if dead at our feet
we'd sit amongst your salt-glazed pots
and sip away whole afternoons in talk.

He wrote inviting me to go and choose
some ring or brooch to remember you by,
but I like things as they are –
the regular deceptions weave you back
into my life, like thread.
Smooth old gold, a glittering stone,
would make your death a permanence,
would cut me off from you too soon.

SUNDAY MORNING

That drizzled morning in despair,
she left him asleep and started walking.
Chance seemed to draw her to the market
and the stall. A copper box.
The grating on its lid was chased
with chrysanthemums, the handle was brass.

But why should she buy him anything?
'Know what it is?' the dealer asked.
'It must be oriental. Incense perhaps?'
He smiled: 'It's for crickets,
the Chinese loved to hear them sing.'
She counted out her money.

How on earth did they catch them?
Poor, wild crickets, cramped, in darkness . . .
She saw their prison swinging from a hook,
caught the frantic arias above the chink
of porcelain teabowls and the tap,
tap, tap of tiny pointed slippers.

She clasped the package to her
and waited for the bus to take her home.
Would the curtains still be drawn?
And how could this box – or anything –
make a difference to their life?
Yet through a copper grid the crickets sang . . .

ONCE UPON A TIME

A woman bade goodbye to the man she truly loved
and stayed with the one she didn't.
Roses covered the porch, the family swelled
and she sighed. The trees bore fruit
the children fled the nest, and she sighed.
The cockerel was eaten by a fox, the dog
and two cats died and, of course, she sighed.
But at last her tears ceased to flow.

Something had been forged out of all that pain –
a friendship, nothing more, with the man
whose love she had spurned, and a garden, shared . . .
Then, one fine autumnal day, when shiny apples
plumped on branches, smoke curled upwards
from the drifts of amber leaves her husband burned
and *snip, snip*, said her clippers to the lavender,
she stopped to smell a perfect late pink rose.

Like a dog that waits for its master's precious tread
she threw back her head and listened.
It was the returning sound of love.
She flung down the clippers, tore off her gloves
and raced out through her prison's gates,
into the road and the traffic of life.
Ending A says she met her man and was never sorry
and ending B says she was liberated by a lorry.

I DO NOT WANT THE CEILING
OF THE SISTINE CHAPEL

I hated you; I confess I hated you,
for tossing away your talent, after art school,
for marrying, for settling down and having me.
I watched you live your life vicariously,
and dissipate that gift on the family.

Once, as you stirred a vat of marmalade,
I challenged you and you shrugged and said:
'Obviously I didn't have the drive . . . '
But pestered by my own poor demons,
I – your child – refused to understand.

Now you're gone I look everywhere for traces
of your being – in places that you loved,
old letters, my own reflected face; I ransack
the stash of memories, finding nothing.
And almost giving up, I turn to your art.

The student oils depress me – that grimy portrait
of my bearded, glum great-grandfather,
whose canvas someone put a finger through,
the stiff flowers that hung in the Royal Academy . . .
but then I come across the sketch-books.

You never went on holiday without your paints.
I remember you, perching on rocks, in the sun . . .
I hear the tinkle of your brush in the water jar,
watch you lick the sable point and as it darts
across your knees, I fret again to see the picture.

Suddenly I understand. There's joy and life here –
in the white shelved bay with a placid sea,
the terracotta bowl of oranges and lemons,
the gaggle of beach umbrellas, that yucca
bursting into flower beneath a southern sky –

and my grievance crumbles like that ochre dust
on the snaking goat track up the mountains.
Great art – all that struggle and pain – may lie
elsewhere; who cares, for now I have my mother back.
I do not want the ceiling of the Sistine Chapel.

I HAVE TAKEN THE SUITS
AND SHOES TO OXFAM

I slide into his life
glide into his geriatric ways.
I wind his wheezing grandfather clock,
I feed his birds and goldfish,
I sit for hours in his chair
and watch the fountain dribble.

I scrutinize the lists he made
on the backs of envelopes,
stare at the portrait of my mother,
feel the prick of his loneliness
and the cramp of his despair.
My world stops here.

I flush away his pills – the purple,
red and white – as I'm told to do.
I dispose of the two sets of teeth.
I dust and mop, though God knows why,
and find that fatal red cigar
beneath his bed, (they took the gun).

Yet there's no letter left for me
in his tiny, spider's writing,
no age-bruised hand extended
to a daughter . . . nothing to hang

my desolation on. But then
he knew that I'd know why.

I trim his patch of meadow grass,
yank bindweed from the border,
and dredge up stalactites of slime
from his pond. Green entrails cling,
like memories, to the ramps of brick
he made for voles and hedgehogs.

He gave me life and now gives death,
his own. Full circle. His ending
seems as random and promiscuous
as my existence. And so I sit
and wait for great tits and the gleam
of his ever circling fish.

I have taken the suits and shoes to Oxfam.

Bibhu Padhi

TAKING CARE OF THE DEAD

Entering my room this morning I found
our family cat and her child sitting
on my table, their four eyes staring
at the bundled-up thing lying in a corner.
The mouse had been trapped and taken care of.

On seeing me enter, they quietly descended
to the floor, stood for a while amid books
that lay all about the carpet, and then
walked out of the room. I went near the thing
only recently lulled to sleep, a spot of kiss
still red and fresh on its upper neck.

This certainly isn't the best time to begin, I thought.
The dead lay there still, unattended and bleeding
its last drop of life. I held its still-warm tail
and while it looked towards the earth, moved
out of the room to find a proper place
to hide last night's death in.

The cat and her child waited outside, attentive
like responsible gods, as if they knew
where the dead must go so that life might begin once more.
I threw the dead where in the backyard
other unwanted objects lay: envelopes
without their contents, rotting leaves,
skins of fruits we peeled months ago.

Mother and child followed me with sure steps;
they knew where the dead went. Putting their mouths
to the slender neck, they tore it apart, leaving
the head and the tail in an arbitrary assembly
of memories, buried or only half-seen.

Minutes later they were in my room again,
sniffing and smelling near the dark corner
where the dead lay a while ago, licked the place
clean. The dead had left the room altogether,
reinvested now with the habit of daily tears.

POWER-CUT IN MARCH

It has been happening
for the past four years, beginning
each March. The water-level behind
the high embankment on Mahanadi
drops to its bottommost and fails to work
the hydraulic turbines anymore.
The officials make polite statements,
offer similar instances of failure
in the neighbouring states.

The late afternoon moves into
the darkness of waiting.
Inside the rooms, the lantern light
seems enough. The shadows
are everywhere, on the walls
and the high ceilings.

We like it in a sense. On the open terrace,
lying on the reed mat and waiting for the lights
to come back later than the appointed hour,
we watch the sky. The stars
are brighter than ever, Jupiter's light steadier,
after a long time the shooting stars catch the eye.

'How do they stay so still unless
their hands support each other?
Is the star out there, faint
as the lantern light, grandmother's?'
My son's questions are many
and remain unanswered.
I count his pulse, and then mine;
their measured beats link us to the stars.

And then, strictly following yesterday's
weather forecast, the nimbus clouds
from the north gather, the breeze

gets heavier, minute by minute.
The first large drops of spring rain
fall on our faces, we move within.

The same rain, we guess, must be falling now
at the point where Mahanadi originates
among forests and boulders, seven hundred miles
above us, in Madhya Pradesh, making the water
rise at the right places. The television
announcer had said: 'Large convective clouds
seen from the satellite picture
suggest uninterrupted rain for
the most part of the rest of the week.'

The afternoon will no more move
into the evening as it did today
and for the past several days;
we'll forget to use the terrace once more.
As the rain comes down louder than ever,
through the windows we try to locate
the particular stars, which now seem
to be suffering the bewildered space,
their once-joined hands separated now
by the clouds and the gathering dark.
Ny eyes strain to retrieve that one star
which, on the western sky, had become
my grandmother to my son, now obscured by the rain.

THE GRAVEDIGGERS

He was a good Christian, but we knew
that it would be a day of fog and cold wind,
a bad day for death or burial.

We looked for the caretaker everywhere.
He was gone, so too were his diggers.
They had taken a day off to be among
the living instead of the unspeaking.
His hut was open. After all,
what was the use keeping it closed?
The dead might appear anytime
and choose to be buried soon.

We gathered the necessary tools
and started working ourselves down.
It was difficult and we were inexperienced.
We had never placed even a twig or leaf
in grounds much softer that this.
The job changed hands, four at a time, until
we could work no more. 'It's solid stone,' someone
remarked, 'and wouldn't yield at all.'
He was right, and we lacked the right skill.

It took us five hours of strain and sweat
to reach two feet down.
Now all seven of us worked with a vengeance,
but our hands and feet were getting weaker.
And then, quietly, out of the unresponsive stone,
one sleeping eye appeared, and then another, and then
the sharp nose, the thick lips set amid
a face that seemed familiar and near.

We now worked hard and quick at it, and soon
it showed itself, every little detail intact
as in a sculptor's granite dream.
Our friend lay above us, waiting to be laid

five feet below, away from the cold.
The figure below was a little too familiar
to be ignored, as if waiting for us
through centuries of denudation and faith.
But we knew it waited for something else too.
We lowered our friend into the grave
and stood in prayer for a minute or so.
With the sweat still large on our foreheads,
we closed the grave and returned
to our homes through the fog, now slowly clearing.

BURIAL IN SUMMER

Returning home through the sun's midsummer
afternoon heat, I found a housesparrow
on the bedroom refrigerator, its small head
dipped into the foot of the alarm-clock,
its tail pointing at a thin angle to my eye.
The clock hands read twenty minutes past noon.
What could a sparrow do with time
and the humid heat of a windless day?
I put on the fan, thinking the breeze
would wake it from its worthless sleep inside
a house where sleep couldn't achieve much.
But it stayed where it stayed and didn't even
turn its head from the ticking moments.
I waited a minute or so, put off the fan;
something told me that it wasn't so.
I placed my fingers as softly as
those fingers could be placed:
the body was warm still, but I knew
it 'was the heat retained from summer's plenty.
The curious red ants swarmed about its beak where
it touched the clock; they had found
their unintended prey. I took it up, now hard and finished
as one made from fine-grained clay and displayed
at so many makeshift roadside shops. I went down
to the garden and dug with my fingers a proper grave
near a place under the *champak* tree where
grandmother's bones rested. And while other birds
sang elsewhere in the garden, I placed it in and filled
the tiny grave with earth and stone, away from
time's hard gaze, inside earth's darkness where
one season or the change of seasons wouldn't matter.
Perhaps it is there still, dreaming of quick
impulsive flights and enjoying
its long rest, beside grandmother's bones.

PUNISHING MY SON

for William Stafford

He stood before me in a cold cruel posture,
holding back everything. He knew what it was
that would've given me my freedom
and, he wouldn't give me that.

We kept looking at each other, straight in the face,
while I thought of which other, subtler trick
would be able to find him out from the surrounding dark
so we might find ourselves once again together.

He wouldn't let himself out of the dark.
He just stood there, waiting for the next
word, his small eyes shining
like a cat's, through the dark.

Which other invention would also be
a perfect invitation? I had invented enough
and failed. My freedom was now bound
to his imprisonment and my own commands.

Slowly I picked up the clues. 'If you do it again,
you'll have to sleep for a whole week in the other room
alone, in the dark, with pillows on either side
instead of me and your mother.'

He stood for a while in childish disbelief, as if
my words came from another land, before he
drew closer, his tentative fingers trying to reach out
to my cheeks, his face leaning to my bare chest.

He let out what he had held back till now.
I could feel the warm tears.

THE EARTHQUAKE

The morning it arrived

we looked at our costly watches,
wondered at the rare miscalculation of
the town's usually efficient astrologer.

We traced its humble origin
to acts of pride and violence
committed a long time ago.

We told ourselves: 'There are
other worlds yet, other spaces,
where human beings can find

sufficient room
for all the many sins
of the body and the soul.'

We felt the insidious
vibration of God's anger
at our poor little doorsteps.

In a fit of human rage, we promised
to build houses that'll keep their cool
during sly unsympathetic weather.

We came out of our homes and saw
the planets giving birth
to other, larger planets.

We said: 'After this invasion of faith,
mankind shall learn to stand
erect and upright again;

once again God shall ascend
our ill-lit altars
and allow us to pray.'

That evening, while we were trying
to gather up our exploded faith,
we saw the stars and the moon in tears.

We sat down and prayed.

MIGRATORY CRANES NEAR LAKE CHILKA

for Robert Penn Warren

The lake is shining and quiet, –
from this point on the road
that cuts across mountain forests, –
its nearer borders a ring of foaming surf.
The fugitive birds are already here –
tenants of the warm sky and thick clusters
of rocky hills that the islands hold.
They've left winter behind four thousand miles
of land and sea, in the gathering snow.
They find their home here, in the vast expanse
of salt water that remains the same
throughout the year.
Summer has just ended, but its warmth
still lingers in the clear mountain air.
The birds fly over the lake, around
its several islands, scattered up to
the Bay of Bengal, dip into its depths and flick
the water off their shimmering wings and rise,
their broad bodies carrying the refracted sun
all about the territory that the eye beholds.
They are getting their first touch of sea water
which waits for them this time every year
in a soft welcoming gesture. From here
it all seems so near, like a framed picture

that shall never leave the gaze of
the attentive eye, sharing in what the eye desires.
The birds are once again here.
Seven months later, in April, haunted by
the nostalgia of yet another summer,
they shall return to the wide plains of Siberia.
From this point on the road that cuts through
mountain forests, I can only stand and watch
their long north-western flight, in huge flocks.
The eye would turn back and find only
the framed picture, hanging blank
on the wall of another summer.

A WOUND ELSEWHERE

Not here, not here, not this, not here.
It is one of so many things
that I've failed to locate this year.
I face questions about my declining health
from anxious lips;
the answers remain ordinary, familiar.
Nothing has happened, no one will know.

It isn't the migraine that I get
every third day, nor the wish to lie
on the bed, face in the pillow, when
the moon is fully awake. It isn't because
I remember my father who died young,
nor the recent nervous breakdown
of my still-young mother. It isn't because
I don't receive letters from friends
who once were dear to me and are now lost
among the city crowds of Calcutta or Bhopal;

nor because my son is growing up and would like
to have his own friends and spend his time
in ways that may not be mine; nor my brothers
who live elsewhere among their own
commitments, building up their own homes;
nor even my wife's frequent neuralgia.

From deep within the night, the dreams come,
clad in white, clean as dawn's light, wherein
familiar figures fluently move as birds in flight.
I wake up, my hands on my chest, and see
my wife and child close to me, their warmth
accompanying my body's winter. I know
I ought to believe in things that lately
I've been losing faith in, but it is
so different from all of them, so distant!
I'm only being ambiguous and rhetorical,
they complain. I should know better so I might
put it across, in plain English.
But it is there somewhere, where words
are afraid to go, as some yet unexplored spot
in the outer space.

I place my fingers on every little object
that I've shared with others, on every
single grief that I've suffered with myself,
deep within the dark night of others' sleep.
But not this, not there, not this, not here.
No one knows, no one would know.
It is always some *other* place –
the hurt stealing into the night from there.

William Palmer

'THE STARS ARE THE INFORMERS OF THE SKY'

(Mandelstam)

I am the only thing that you fear.
All night the temperature falls;
the stars, occluded, break at last
into three o'clock, tree-brakes separate
in moonlight, and two badgers pass
over the empty road.

Your hands are raised, the lamp casts them far
and huge, and huge they move on the still
blue faces of portraits,
papered walls. Silence leans as you lean;
a black cabinet disclosed by one curtain,
night defaced, unpeaceful.

THE PHOTOGRAPHS OF WALKER EVANS

The negroes at the barber's
face the light, that comes,
that takes a white square
church, turns it to a monument.

The child with the little cock
who dare not take
a step for fear of falling
– hands reach out – has

already seen the picture perched
about the fireplace, birds searched
for in the trees, and shot down, that
the light is everywhere.

Charms
and birdscares on the telephone wires;
forks, grandmother's photo and black Fords;
a hole in the fireplace – 'Please be Quite . . . '

dyslexia of dialect, despair;
the harness hung on the open door.

THE MIRROR OF THE DOVE

Like lovers to
their sudden futures,
under Mill Bridge
the seamless waters
part, the Dove in two;

the weir fall-races,
turbulences,
crests, white undersided,
where our faces
cannot show, show

division
undivided – a vision
of the turning mill,
veined water running in
the hollow wheel,

the song's partition; it is still.

Silence between
grace and order, silence between
the arches of air
and water, silence
far falling where

over the other
arm of the river
that flowing, glistens,
Venus the lover
of musicians,

makers of words,
dancers, the bird's
stone mouth,
throat flickering, fords
in the South.

THE MAP OF LOVE

The glass comes dry
just after rain
the roofs dry
blue, grey-blue and grey.

The gold clocks hiss
before they chime;
an island echoes
off the land . . .

The chart returns
by woods in fall,
bears trees as ferns.
The meadows walk

in green and rise
in finger-
prints of giants
whorled.

       Blue water's
paper on the bed,
your island white,
its river red . . .

The estuary's white
tower lays down
a shadow to water
earth will turn

over the drowned
light-streaming town.

COLONIAL SPRING

Layer on layer the water froze, unfroze
the whale and bear and arched-backed lovers'
shapes the water made

(you see them on the blankets that they weave;
benign and sacred monsters of the lake).

The weavers' bodies rot, hidden by the forest.
The fresh white stones are for our dead;
the moving life in blue shoots on the back
the shadows of tall grass.

THE TYRANNY OF I

Do you remember the story of poor Mishka?
– Mishka who read his creation,
full of nicotine, wine and passion,
to Babel – and it was worthless,

secondhand – a thousand hands
had done the thing before, and will do.
My room was long and slanted to the window.
If I came in too drunk I would disturb

myself by walking into the ceiling,
which would heave up, absorbent with its rot.
All day I would go out and did not.
A girl's legs twined about an arse below me.

Evening all afternoon, and then the real evening
came down. Girls, wine and snow.
The local moon shone in my barrow;
working on words before the stars, unseen, gave out.

MY DAUGHTER, RESTLESS TONIGHT

My daughter, restless tonight,
comes troubled from some dream.
My shadow crosses the dim light
that from the landing lights her room.

Her hair is damp, her eyes
see nothing, open, but their fear.
I am her father, tall and wise,
trying to talk her back to here.

It must be – it is all she knows
– that somehow our world of gesture,
noise, implacably roaring, overthrows
the silence, order, promised her.

Her nightmare rides, never
I pray to join with ours.
What is her innocent fretting fever
to the burning cities, discontinued stars?

ARIEL AND CALIBAN

The fault is this –
the actor chosen
to play the monster
always *can* act,
at least get a laugh
wrapped in the sack
with Trinculo.
But, oh,
the one who gets Ariel
– a composite libel –
is the old boy
of a young company
much afflicted by gesture
– the thinning crown–
just thirty-four – poised
on his Mercury
toes, immortally bound-
ing golden man –
a sort
of shot-
down
      Peter Pan.

Trip, trip, thump, trip
he runs (stage left) and looks –
golden leotarded,
hollow bum-cheeked,
one arm outstretched,
poor big-balled sod –
slightly retarded.

A TRIP TO THE BLIND ASYLUM

A narrative for girl's voice

1

'Curable – if taken soon enough in hand . . . '
She took my hand
and led me through the garden
– starting to scent –
handing me up the carriage step
– the coldness of her fingers –
with Henry's hot hand pulling.
Then mother settling
beside me; beside herself,
not knowing what to say.

2

Now I am taken, feeling
as though I take *them*
unwillingly, through darkness to darkness.
The world too far, too near
in the feel of the seat, the breathing of Henry,
the start, the heavy ring
of horse's hooves, the brush
of cool air now we are going.
And I am flying through night
on a midsummer morning;
an echoing head; my body
a tadpole's, insignificant,
to be ignored for the present.
A head carried through air,
cutting swiftly through air,
air a felt presence,
a net tightened.

3

Travelling with Henry,
I know he is looking at me
and that he smiles.
All is a thick velvety black
pushed aside in
tiny, exquisite
brilliant corners,
a huge mirror facing the sun
its back silver finely scratched.
'It's sunny,' says Henry. 'Again.'

'We are passing – oh
such a pretty wood. Oh, I am sorry . . . '
And I feel mother move on the seat
in her sorrow.
'Tell me the colours.'
'Green and brown,' says Henry. 'Brown and green.'
Why does he hate me?
Now I shall never see him again.
Mother will die.
And if Henry should visit he will,
year after year,
bore, go bald
talk through poor teeth;
mask his voice
with his young face forever.
Now I am glad of this carriage.
It holds me
and Mother and Henry
and the disappeared fields,
all the stopped faces.

4

Now we are turning.
The sound of the wheels,
rhythm of hooves changes.
My mother explains the high stone pillars,
iron gates, porticoed house, girls
walking hand in hand
on the straight paths of the garden.
We go on a short time and we stop.
'Miss Race? Mrs Race?'
a neat small
buzzingly ecstatic voice
like a tired bee.
'Yes. Yes?' says my mother.
Another cold hand helps me down.

5

We are mounting steps.
I stumble.
'Take my arm, my dear.'
No. Thank you. I will feel the door.
The hard wood rising
cool, with a little smoothed out
painted over indentation
where my fingers grip.
It is a liberation you feel
when you know you are here
to be kept.

6

Never to be let go now.
To move in my skull
as freely as the world
this smooth invisible house
– each open window
an arithmetic square enclosing space;
the warm broad curves
of the balustrade.
I have years to learn
these Euclidities of darkness,
the mysteries of dress,
to read by the Moon.

Petra Regent

SHOES

Why is it
that I no longer love
your shoes?
Such little things
I used to drag
into my empty hours
to think about.
Or stare
at your familiar bookshelves,
watch the way you write
your name –
the beautiful encasement
of you within inanimate things.

I remember the jumper
you lent me
in autumn rain,
and how I surreptitiously kissed
its armpit smell.

Now all is gone.
I can't stand your shoes.
They're all pointed and wrong.
Why is it
that I no longer love
your shoes?

DAWN BEFORE COLOUR

Upon waking
my room has become a different country,
a cold clutter of unfamiliar shadows,
a sullen province entered only in dreams.

The landscape through my window
hangs in limbo,
like a pale face,
a visiting moon.
Fields are washed grey
as my sleep-twisted sheets.

The back of the chair
heaped with crumpled clothes
stands mute
bearing its burden.
I am in occupied territory
where every slight step
sets the floorboards creaking
like a landmine.

Features of the past
are erased
by the heavy mortars
and constant machine-gun fire
of experience.
They have defaced the street
of innocence
where I once used to live.

Collective terror drags us
further back than that,
beyond the swastika
and the washing of hands
to a dark forest
peopled by fallen angels
and heraldic lions with sad eyes.

A train rumbles.
Light reveals the grain in the wall
like a magician.
A slip of paper on the table
shines like spilt blood.

NORTH

In the far north
the falling tern twists
a parabola of sky
like a blue scarf
upon its wings.

The wind shuffles shadows
in a random sequence
of sunshine and rain.

The tundra transfers its allegiance
to the seasons at a moment's grace –
one moment forbidding
as a grey November dawn,
the next, shimmering
with the spectral luminosity
of northern light
dancing like fireflies,
transient as the passage of love
across the landscape of the human face.

The north seduces me
as you once did
upon that dark tapestry
of bare peat and filigree moss.
Your kiss elemental
as the plaintive cry
of an arctic bird.
(A messenger from the ice.)

GREENFINCHES AT DAWN

Do not despise the moss.
Such tenacity deserves respect.
In every monotony of wall
there is a green-slitted eye.
Pouched cushions lie
deep in woods, tempting
lost souls to sleep. Moss
softens bare rock on heath
and empty wastes, turns stone
to gentleness, as rain beautifies
steel to rust.
And the air is thick
with the same awe
as mushrooms and magic.

I went in the dawn
to watch goldfinches in the graveyard.
The silence was as deep as the pitch
where the wind is hurling hardest,
yet the wind's eye is still.

The birds slipped in and out of the yews
like gleaming gloves into a secret pocket.
And the sky was still unopened.
I was the child in the secret attic,
staring at past beauty, thick with dust,
longing to touch, but not knowing how.

DEVON BEDROOM

Do you remember
waking
as the first light
crept in from the moor?
Pale as mist, delicate and clear
as steel. Chiselled and tempered
by cold winds.

You'd thrown your pomegranate beard
upon the pillow next to me.
We lay warm beneath an autumn fall
of blankets,
secure as woodland creatures,
wintering-out.

Beyond the window, the sea
ensnares the land:
woos the indifferent shore –
will never cease to run with the moon.
And bending inland from the strand,
man-carved lanes wind, hidden from gales,
hedged for cattle, and the solitary whistle
of the herding boy.

Before the tides have run too far
up the morning's sands, already dressed
with gifts
by the amaranthine attentions of the waves,
we must run out to watch
the gulls soar high with a scream on their wings,
taste salt upon the lips, that is not blood.
Before the sun has mounted the garden fence
we must run down to the sea.

POEM WRITTEN BEFORE THE FIRE

And we shall harvest stillness
in the hiss of flame.
Bring it in
in soft bales
as night falls
upon the fields.

We gaze upon transparent things –
untamed dreams and mongol faces leap up
to dwarf us.
Lulled by turning page
and the familiar companion
of four walls, we allow
our hearth to kindle delight.

Outside a lone bird calls
of desire
for its own kind.
In that thicket of darkness
we cannot know if such a call
goes unheard.

SEND ME YOUR WARMTH

Send me your warmth on a postcard, my love.
The smell of your skin has gone from the sheets,
though I've not washed them for months.
Your absence is an ominous thread
worked into the tapestry of time,
prelude to a final solitude.

I taste your lips
in the bruise of apples.
Smell your hair
in the acerbic corruption of leaves.
Touch your skin
warm as the late marrow's smooth flank.
Hear your step
in every cat's trespass.

The dark earth I turn
is your love.
I lay it bare
to the frost and the wind.

JERUSALEM ARTICHOKES

Little brown wrinkled roots,
smelling of earth and mould.
Tiny phallic buds,
cool, and warted,
touch like a man's cheek.
Fields full of stones
beneath the lee of the rain.
Hawthorn and ash surround
with blade-light needles of war.

Artichoke from Jerusalem.
Manna of the silica glare
of the sun. Delight
to Ruth, alone and hungry
in the wide dust.
First offering of Cain
to the Lord.
Sown, harrowed, reaped,
moving to the seasons' rhythms,
the genesis of furrow and fallow field.
And the Lord had not respect.

And granger, peasant, serf,
share-cropper, crofter
inherit the earth and hell
in the absence of God.
He did not touch these things:
forest and field,
familiar as boots,
but tied and staked
to tenant, yeoman, landlord.
Feud and narrow strip.
Fallow order, and crowded Norman lands.

THE GREAT YARMOUTH EXPRESS

Families already exhausted by the early hour,
children sticky with too many bribes,
slump in the heat of the fly-ridden train.
Strangers smile, finding
their sufferings and expectations shared.

The train rumbles.
Sun lacquers the city we leave behind.
Fields lie, sculptured by the wind,
burnished by the sun –
a still-life at sea, the green waves
poised in defiance of natural law –
until the harvest brings them down.

Beyond the window, the tide
of new houses spreads –
never recedes,
like a fatal disease.
Preserving perhaps a few chosen things
stranded upon the future's shore:
a weed-choked stream, or straggling copse,
the church whose mossed graves
will soon be manicured and mown.

But at the seat of infection
in the city we've left behind,
an invading army silently
stakes its claim.
The pioneers are already here –
silken parachutes of willowherb descend
to colonize wasteland and crumbling stone.
Ragwort appears at bus-stops overnight.
Bindweed slips
through cracks in paving stones,
and covers them in blooms of white.
Graffiti of anarchist and tyrant alike

are replaced by the hieroglyphics
of the vegetable world.

The tide of builder's rubble and earth
spills like a dark wave upon a field
lost to tomorrow's child.
But in the city's decaying heart,
an emerald forest grows.

THE PEACH THAT GREW

I am eating the peach
that grew in your garden,
ripened by late sun –
the last careless gift of the year,
like a child born after much longing.

Tasting of floods, honey,
and bitter reeds –
biblical elements these,
found beneath a fenland sky.

Now it's October
the gulls venture inland,
black-masked
like pantomime villains.
I've heard them screaming
above the cathedral spire.

Your cheek brushes mine.

Oktay Rifat

*Translated by Ruth Christie
and Richard McKane*

NOT ME

Am I that little child
Schoolbag on back,
Pockets bulging with marbles,
Dreaming of cops and robbers?

Is that really me? Sweating and gulping water,
Falling ill?
Where's the fever I had?
Where's the one who cried by my bed?

If this sailor's shirt is mine
Then why are the sleeves too short?
This is your glove, you say,
Look, it won't fit my hand.

Where's my kite with its frilly tail?
My wooden sword and my trumpet?
These pictures are not like me,
I must be a different man.

I'm another person – quite different –
That child is another child.
And the writer of these lines
Lived only for a moment.

Ruth Christie

THE EMBRACE

Warm me this night,
O my trust in freedom
Wrap me warm
Against my mattress thin and blanket torn;
Out there is unimaginable cold and wind,
Outside – oppression
Torture
Out there – death.
O my trust in freedom
Enter deep
Warm me through this night,
On my palm a place is ready
For your hands,
On my thighs a place
To lean your knees.
Enclose me,
Sheath me,
Wrap me warm,
O my trust in freedom
Wrap me warm this night.

Ruth Christie

FREEDOM HAS HANDS

1

Our horses galloped foaming
to the calm sea.

2

What is this flight? Is it the dove's
joy of freedom?

3

It was forbidden to kiss, did you know,
forbidden to think,
forbidden to defend the work force.

4

They've picked the fruit from the tree
and they sell it in the market
for as much as they can get,
labour's broken branches on the ground.

5

Light is blinding, they say,
and freedom is explosive.
Arsonists smash our lamps
and with oily rags set fire to freedom.

As soon as we reach out, they want an explosion,
and they want us to catch fire when we light the flame.
There are mine-fields,
bread and water wait in the darkness.

6

Freedom has hands,
eyes, feet;
to wipe the bloody sweat,
to look at tomorrows,
heading straight for equality.

7

I'm the cage, you are the ivy;
tangle, tangle as much as you are able!

8

Love of freedom is this:
once you're tempted there's no escape,
it's a habit that never gets old,
a dream that is truer than reality.

9

The brave herdsmen of the flow of history,
the workers, bees of the universe's beehive;
milling round black bread,
brothers who bring freedom to our world.
By that bread the mind is roused from sleep,
our endless night dawns with that bread;
people attain independence with that sun.

10

This hope is the door to freedom,
half open to happy days.
This joy is the light of happy days,
gently, timidly its rays strike us.

Come people of my land, show yourselves
like a budding branch at the door of freedom,
and behind you the sky is brotherly blue.

Richard McKane

THE RAINS

Then the rains began, the acrobats left,
The traces of tents were erased from the plain.
Orange-painted boy, blue-breasted girl,
What became of them? How fast they vanished!
A smile from summer lingered on the walls,
Dead photographs were blown about the street.
They flew rather than walked, their hands
Wide open with the sun.
Pensive and sad
They urged us to lightness.
Prudent and skilled were they, we absent-minded,
Careless, trailing their dreams.
From now, whatever is,
Is empty, dirty, rotting-soft.
The sky with its regal mountains of cloud,
Purple and round, rough as the sea,
Dragging the migrant birds by the hair,
Is moving like a hostile army overhead.
    The rains have begun.

Ruth Christie

A CRAFTY GIPSY

He made hundreds of whistles from the willow branch,
a crafty gipsy in a horse cart.
We went down to the gipsy camp in the meadow,
with stolen zinc and daisies.
A sunny wind was blowing, the weather was warm.

On roads humping down, overlooking the sea,
on both sides of us mallows, and patience;
lie out on the wet grass if you want, walk about if you want.
Tin-Tin the sheepdog is following us,
he stops, pisses, sniffs the bottom of the pebbles.

My tree rustles at the slightest breeze,
a crow drops from the top of the pine,
my inside leaps like lightning.
The sky, three or four clouds, evening strangeness,
what else have we got left in this lying world?

Richard McKane

ON SILENT SHORE

One day poems finish
sea-urchins octopi survive
sweet basil behind glass

one day hopes finish
a horse cart in the shade
the mare suckles its foal

I saw all these things
the mare the coffee house the vine

you in your short skirt
unaware of its significance
were looking at me
as for me with unattainable speed
I was scything the night that had begun into two

I looked: the sea had finished
the sand was bloody
the doors creaking
the roads the narrow road the pebbly roads
like the lifeless fingers of a dead hand

I saw these things with my own eyes
on silent shore
the blue seagulls' cries falling about me

Richard McKane

1619

A comet could be seen that year
a bloody light cluster in the sky
curved as a scimitar
from east to west
there was a huge-headed snake
hanging over Istanbul

Istanbul was terrified.

Richard McKane

GHOST

When I'm dead I'll come
I'll leap on a stone and come
I'll shine in the candle of your room
Behind the wet glass
Through the heart of the shadows
I'll creep
And wait till all's quiet
I'll not stay for the light of day
I'll come with the rain
Wait for me
I'll be there
When the hour strikes
When the Other is gone
When night descends
I'll come.

Ruth Christie

TREE ANECDOTE

That year the cherry blossoms of the spring
Instead of staying to fruit
Were dropping off untimely –
The garden was deserted,
I was not there, nor you,
And these lines perhaps had not yet been written.

A horseman came from the South,
He looked at the blossoms on the ground,
He hung his whip on the tree,
He turned his horse's head and went.

Ruth Christie

ON SEA-URCHIN ROCK

The fish that are my friends
I harpooned them and threaded them on the wire
and sold them
at the fish-seller's counter

That day in the open on sea-urchin rock
my knees all bloody
a little bream on my harpoon
I skinned it and bit into it
with glee

I bit into the meat of my people on sea-urchin rock
into the sun the salt nature I bit
all the folk songs of the Anatolian poets
especially my Yunus Emre and my Pir Sultan Abdal.

Like painting in a paint book
I mixed blue for the sea
sunk into indigo
I was a crab an octopus
I opened the door of the 40th room
with that missing skeleton key
I felt the existence of my existence
on sea-urchin rock in the sun

Richard McKane

Valerie Thornton

ON THE UNDERGROUND (2)

A bird child hops into the carriage
perches on a seat
and chirps happily at us all.
Dark hair spiked like a crested crane
wild eyes too far apart
the corner skin drawn down
akin to a nictating membrane.

He has a small curved beak of a nose
and screeches in delight
beating curled fists
off the lurching cushions,
bright eyes flickering
from face to fascinated face.

Beside him, a young woman
her jaw horizontal as an eagle's
guards her offspring
with sharp unblinking gaze.

FAIRIES IN THE FOG

It was so exciting
when the end of the road disappeared.

Wrapped in scarves and mitts
(thumb free to wriggle,
fingers webbed in a woollen wedge
neatly grafted by mother)
water-proof, chill-proof,
fleece-lined ankle-boots,
brown, with stiff zips up the front,
firm on my favourite pavement,
glittering like a black fruit pastille.

My feet ate up the road to school
and friendly lumps filtered through the fog
and laughed and jumped and yelled
at the strangeness of their voices,
till school loomed, tall and grey
like a ship, with yellow lights.
We made plasticine fairies all day then
or so it seemed.

Later, our physics teacher tells us
'Fog is a colloid.'
We note it without passion
for the next test.

Now in the city
life is so much sharper.
The fogs have lifted
with the last of the ships,
the rain scratches diamante spikes
on the window,
boots keep my feet cold and wet,
ice is vicious and deceitful.

But a fog has settled in our souls
in the muddle we make of our lives,
in our short-sighted decisions,
our purblind freedom of choice.

The end of the road has long disappeared.
We should not have forgotten
the way to make plasticine fairies.

PERHAPS YOU ARE NOT MY FUTURE

I answer the phone
because maybe it's not you.

Your shrill hello
peaks beyond the valium.

You talk about the weather
in a monologue minutes long.

'Of course, children don't like vinegar.'

I can't let it pass
and we argue
for interminable minutes.

Everything an argument.

At last, the point of your call,
saved carefully for days –
yet another trivial irrelevance
I neither need nor want
to know.

You are too dry for tears,
too raw to heal,
too ragged to bind yourself.
Gangrene of the mind.

If it weren't your own mother,
resentful in a home,
it would be something else.

I cannot help.
Your inarticulate calls for help
only make me angry,
guilty,
sad.

The cat climbs on to me, purring,
and plays with the coiled cord
which still tethers me to you.

LILI MARLENE NIGHTS

A small golden star
on a militaria stall
catches my eye.
An old man sits behind the medals.
'How much is that?'
'Two-fifty – it's an Africa star.'
He takes two pounds.
Peels off three, for my fiver.
'Whose was it – do you know?'
'No idea – just regulation issue.'

I tuck it away in my purse
and walk off with someone's memories,
someone's Lili Marlene nights
in the interminable desert,
someone's sacrificed years
and scarified emotions,
reduced by fifty pence.

MASON, NOT ORANGEMAN

He takes a long time
to paint his new windows orange,
this little old man
who lives across the street.
His hand leaves shaky lines
against the old green pointing
and smears his age
on the soft pink sandstone.

Even the windowsills are orange
when he's finished,
and inside he hangs orange curtains
to match something.

He gets up slowly at ten
and watches all sorts of colours
all day on his television.

Sometimes he watches
the little Italian girl play
in her garden below here;
sometimes he creeps along the street
with his little tan shopper,
hair neat and white,
shoes polished orange.

Nothing changes, but he does not know
he can be seen against the frosted glass
of his toilet, or he would put up
a little orange net curtain.

Last week an ambulance whisked him away
and buried him somewhere.
Neighbours talk in sombre tones
of the late ship's carpenter,
mason, not orangeman,
his wife gone these fifteen years.

The boy who lives on the same landing
leaps up and down and shouts
'The old man's dead!'
while his mother doesn't seem to hear.

Then men come quickly and park a big blue van
on the pavement, and empty the brown furniture
and brown television and everything
except the orange curtains,
in less time than he took
to paint the edge of one window.

The windowsills are still trembling orange
but the space behind the glass is black.
In the garden below
the boy kicks the heads off marigolds.

SILK MOTH GHOSTS

I slip silk on next to my skin.
I used to assume the exotic allusions too.

Yesterday I met the artisans
in a small glass box, in a glasshouse
in the rain.

Milk-pale, furry silk moths
with ragged wings outspread
crawled fluttering on the glass floor.

Benign and plump, unable to eat or fly,
the soft creamy creatures lay three days of eggs.

In a corner, spread-eagled,
a crumpled silk moth.

In another corner, a few limp mulberry leaves,
for greedy green caterpillars preparing to spin
their thousand yards of finest pure silk
like a finger bandage around themselves.

Against the glass wall held by guys of silken thread,
a cocoon with dark fluid seeping out,
ruining the silk.

For my sensual silks, they unspin the cocoons
hundreds of times over.
What do they do with all the half-moths?

I still slip on the sad soft silks
(shantung, tussore, crêpe de chine)
and wonder where the gentle silk moth ghosts
are shivering.

JIMMY GATZ IS GONE

Distress flares hang pink
over Partick.
The towers chime twelve
and two ships call
a rich chord
to the new year
as we kiss
below the wide windows
and the yells.

A man with a sharp black coat
and a long furled umbrella
is crying in tongues to the night.
We cross, crossing the road,
his unlit cigarette white and pleading,
his eyes filled with tears.

We have nothing for him,
but he is Jonathan
lost for many years.

He was younger then, than me,
a blond, blue-eyed Gatsby of a boy,
white and golden in the long hot tennis summers,
on the red dust of Livilands,
where hospital visitors have parked their cars
for years.

Now with haunted and sunken eyes
rimmed red in the headlamps
forlorn in the friendly city
decayed from the student days
a decade ago.

We were always going separate ways;
he has to find a light.

I weep for his darkness
as our black coats merge in goodbye.
His neck, below my hand, is soft and warm.
We wish each other a courteous, happy new year.

Hours later, homing in opposite directions,
opposite sides of the road,
an unsteady dark form
weaves in front of the headlamps
cursing the world in a tongue of his own
smashing his umbrella against a litter bin.

CROSSING OVER

Gran has stopped.

She sits upright
still as Sunday morning
fingers folded in her lap
flowered nightdress falling
from the bones
which are her shoulders.
Her vacant eyes are closed,
her ears are emptied of sounds,
she feels no finger
stroke her fallen cheek.

Yet still she beats on
cursed with the momentum
of ninety-seven years
of breath on breath,
night on night.

Her pupils dance below the lids
dreaming on the other side.

Gerard Woodward

SUFFOLK INTERIOR

And when the brass vase she stole
From Stoke-by-Nayland
Was placed on the dresser

My brother restole it and sold it for scrap,
And when we lowered the venetian blinds
The kitchen was filled with belfry light.

And I remember the infinities of my train set
With the engine furiously figure-eighting
And whose motor smelt of struck flint,

And so my mother's theft made our house
A church, the bench ends of the chair-backs
Felt like knee skin of a child that falls often,

And my father under the ellipse of the lampshade,
Haloed well in reading, knuckles
Digging into the folded wings of his cheek bones,

And the aftermath of the washing-up
Where St Catherine's leper water
Cooled in the red basin,

And the darkness that stayed in the loft
That was roofed in slate slotted
Like feathers on a rook's back

And all the shadows were so old
That if you were to remove the walls
You would have a house of dark air still standing.

WOMAN COMING IN FROM THE RAIN

She enters with the slow elegance
Of a bishop as she hangs her umbrella
On the hook of the hatstand.

Her coat opens like the doors of a church
And releases the flock of smells
That rain has made of her.

And when she enters the kitchen
She is soaked again by dinner-steam
And loves it,

Holds her face over the potato pan
And wears the balaclava of steam
That this gives her.

And her eyelids are full of steam tears
That make her eyes feel huge
As she watches her face through a gap

In the condensation of the mirror.
And she peels off the nerveless skin
Of her gloves

So that she may feel again
And enjoys the wet textures
Of her cat's fur.

And as her body lives with flavours,
What dry sheaves of harvest wheat
Her husband's kiss feels to her.

THE BEREAVEMENT OF MR JONES

Mr Jones was an expert
In the art of origami.
He would thumb through volumes
Of his clean kitchen paper
Before wrapping chips
As though changing a nappy.
He made paper hats
To amuse his nephews.
He enjoyed watching his customers
Pump vinegar on their food
And he refilled each bottle
From a white gallon can.
He was the salt of the earth,
Of this he had sacks and loved
Pouring it into the palm of his hand
Creating a white landscape,
A mining district of peaks
Which a wind from his lips
Would level to plains.
But most important his fish
Which he held by the tail,
Gave them new life in his hot, dark fat.
Poor Mr Jones who was father
To the families of Old Hill,
Fed the children and saw
That they turned into grown-ups.
When his wife died her death
Was announced on a square
Of his kitchen paper
Taped to the window, upper
And lower case letters mixed clumsily.

AN AMERICAN BAPTISM

I

At night we heal
In the white casts
That are our sheets.
What horrific accident have we been in?
Our breathing is sane
But our closed eyes dart
Like the first foetal movements
Of four eggs made of skin.
We are chalk giants
Carved in the uplands of our bed.
The pillows, stuffed with hair,
Seem to have burst to reveal our heads
Tangled like briers germinating
Dreams that complicate us
But frighten out the day diseases
That linger there, our nightmares
Work like the birth fluids
Forming the foetus
In its white room without windows
Until our health can crack the shells,
Our sheets split and we climb out damp
With dream sweat, new and soaked
Our feathers flat and straight.

II

The boats dream the sea
Has become dust and ignited
Like the crackling of burning hair.
The dry dock locks out the real sea
With its iron doors.
The hanging lamp gardens
Shine like stings, like sleep signals
Like flowers that only bloom at night.
They burn deep tubers of light into the water,
The tapering, luminescent roots of the light-flowers.
A nettle garden whose insects
Have bright fangs and build
Steel ladders to pierce
The boat body with arc guns
That kiss with their bright lips
And drool sparks lasciviously.
Rivets are fired in like bullets.
It takes pain to rebuild a ship
They shout in their sleep with steam,
Their steam-shout like the
Substance escaping a burst pillow
Of white feathers, the steam
Forms a thought bubble in the dark air,
The only thought – whiteness.

III

I yawn like a foghorn
As the curtain dust wakes
And glows inwards,
The civilization in the curtains
That parted stand like the fluted columns
Of the entrance to a temple that is morning.
The front door yawns and breathes us out,
The street windows flash open
Their inner lids and watch us
Stride the terrace towards the sea.
Below us the docks are waking
From their troubled sleep,
The cranes lift their necks
Erect as organ pipes.
The boats are steady,
Waiting for the opening of the front door.
We share the experience of being
Rebuilt in painful sleep.
They topple as the sea rushes in
Like a mad mother in her skirts,
And as we walk the breeze from America
Drenches us slowly
Like a baptism of air,
A seal of approval.

TO A POWER STATION

I

You simmer your allotted districts,
Bringing a city's kettles to the boil,
Switched on with index fingers.

Your set of six vases, each huge enough
To make me a tablecloth fly walking
In fear of elbows, are overgrown

With steam, like the flasks
Of film scientists who have discovered
The transformational brew.

II

You are strong under my stairs.
When the fuse blew
And we switched to candles

I played cat's cradle with you,
Threading your silver hair
I sewed you back together again.

(The wet raincoat dripped in the hall)
I flicked the switch by the door
And watched you walk the bulb's tightrope.

III

The pylons crackle like sellotape unwinding.
The power station is tearing its hair out,
Threatening to overheat, turn its bricks red

And scatter them like a child
Tired of its old toys
And wanting attention.

Then we are thankful for the cooling towers
As the power station takes a long
Draught from each and wipes its brow.

IV

Steam is the ghost of water
And rain the ghost of steam
As a flower is the ghost of a seed,

Honey the ghost of flowers
And bees the ghosts of honey.
This then is a ghost house.

I would boil myself if I had a big enough pan,
A Diogenes of the stove, knees to chin, turning
The rings full on, I would happily evaporate.

V

There is a village under wraps,
The church cloaked with oilcloth,
Windows newspapered, only the gardens vulnerable.

Cooling towers, your death is a television event.
I watched it on a day when strong winds
Filled the streets with reading matter.

Christmas arrived early in the village.
The cooling towers fell like gloves,
The thick weather made sills and flowers fat with dust.

FOR THE BIRDS

Next door feed the birds on bread
Throwing it high so it falls in our yard
Like hail. All I see of those next door
Are hands, fingers spread, testing for rain.

As sparrows and tits dine on crumbs
Second volleys fall on them, littering
Their shoulders and backs so that in flight
They shake off their bread like tablecloths.

Next door's breakfasts are behind lock and key.
At dawn I put my ear to the wall
And hear the tap of metal on shell,
The repeated rasp of toast . . .

They blot up yolk with strips of bread,
Scoop out white like Chinese sculptors,
Tear stiff crusts with firm dentures,
Smash their empty egg shells to powder.

It is a frightening thing to hear through our wallpaper,
These alarmingly early breakfasts
Conducted in secrecy by an old couple
Unmarried and childless in a rented house.

Birds wake in a similar fashion,
Teaching their chicks sword swallowing
With a beakful of loaves,
Filling their young with Mother's Pride.

They build their rooms out of newspaper headlines,
Feathers, bread, cellophane,
They rent them from their landlord,
The overseer, their payment is to eat bread.

The elderly always see they have enough bread left.
He buttons his collar, tieless like a priest
And scatters his bread, celebrating the many
Marriages that have happened in his back yard.

His dicky heart flies with the brides,
The newly wed sparrows thankful
For the confetti that falls on them each day,
They build new shells out of it, the future bread eaters,

At night old Mr Something's pipe
Pecks at his ash-tray. I hear it.
I hear the soft blows of his mistress
As she exercises their fat, white pillows.

GRANDFATHER'S ROCKING-HORSE

Her father, the metal bender,
Comes home with hands as scratched
As though he'd been playing with a cat.

He bathes her with his huge hands,
The fingernails white like front teeth,
Skin scored with hairlines of blood.

He grips her like his own huge vice
And stings her with boiling water.
She is for him to fold

As his ringing sheet metal
That creaks in its collapse
And dents his own paws.

Bedtime is her mother's task.
Undressing her with careful hands,
Each button and zip a fruit to be plucked.

In the corner her grandfather's rocking-horse
Grins his Aztec grin
At her nakedness.

The enamel of his teeth peeling,
His mane like the frayed ends
Of a black rope of tar.

Beside him is her stringless violin.
But he has no hands,
Just wooden stumps fixed with bent nails.

He never moves.
Her mother wonders why
She never rides her rocking-horse.

Then sees on her tiny,
Powdered, white buttock
A bruise like a U

THE BRONTË BROTHER

I hear them at night whispering
In their odorous and dark sisterhood,
'How will we get away?' Amid the comfort

Of their shared bed, the moonlight
Making beautiful African hills of the bedclothes.
Their hair seems sewn to their heads,

The beautiful stitching that divides their hair
With such a straight white line,
Their scalps are so pale.

When I see the crowns of their heads on the pillow
It is three faint white lines each at an angle
To the other like half-formed lettering.

And one fears she would be the last to die,
And one uses her clothes
As a feathery shadow. (I lie

In the moonlight in the garden
And I play with the light to see
If I can feel it with my eyes shut

Moving my hand smoothly from shadow to light
And when I feel the moon's heat I open my eyes
And see this exquisite blue candelabra

Hanging in the dark garden air.)
And I imagine them in jewels and metal necklaces
As though an oval mirror had been

Broken over them and they wore its fragments
As acts of heroism.
And I will be drunk on moonlight

As I watch their safe sleep
And the strong smell of their young hair
And their paper white scalps.

My breath passes in clouds over them.
One day I will do a picture of them,
Without their hands of course

And I will fold my painting over
So that the future will make
A ghost cross, a faint cross

Across the face of the painting,
A flaking cross of missing paint
Like the beautiful seams of their heads

That the future will unfold my sisters
As they watch moonlight through a window frame
And see them as bearers of an invisible cross.

Notes on Contributors

SHIRLEY BELL lives on a Lincolnshire cactus farm with her physicist husband and their children. Her poems have been widely published in magazines including *Poetry Review*, *Ambit*, *Critical Quarterly*, *London Magazine* and *The Wide Skirt*, and broadcast on Radio 3's *Poetry Now*. A pamphlet, *Hanging Windows on the Dark*, was published by Wide Skirt Press in 1987. Her work has also appeared in Faber and Faber's *Poetry Introduction 6* (1985), and Rivelin Grapheme's *Six: The Versewagon Poetry Manual* (1985). The poems in this collection have previously appeared in all of these publications.

RUTH CHRISTIE was born and educated in Scotland. She lived and worked in Turkey for some years, and now lives in London where she teaches English literature to American undergraduates. She studied Turkish at the School of Oriental and African Studies.

PATRICIA DOUBELL was born in Dorset. She trained as a dancer and danced professionally, before marrying and farming in Wales. Her poetry was first published in *Adam*, and subsequently in *Tribune*, *Outposts*, *Pick*, *Brief*, *Workshop Magazine*, *Poet International*, *Doves for the 70s* (Corgi Books, 1970) and *The Evans Book of Children's Verse* (Evans Bros, 1972). She has also given many readings and broadcast her poems on Radio 3. Her autobiography *At the Dog in Dulwich* was published by Secker and Warburg in 1986. Acknowledgements are due to the editors of *Adam*, *Workshop Magazine*, *Pick*, *Brief*, and *Doves for the Seventies*, who first published some of the poems in this anthology.

MIMI KHALVATI was born in 1944 in Tehran and grew up on the Isle of Wight. She trained at Drama Centre London and has worked in the UK and in Iran as an actor and director. She now lives in London with her two children. Her poems have appeared in many magazines including *The North*, *PN Review*, *Poetry Durham* and *Poetry Review*, in which some of the poems here were first published. Selections of her work have also been published in *Camden Voices* (Katabasis, 1990), *New Women Voices* (Bloodaxe, 1990) and *Persian Miniatures/A Belfast Kiss* (Smith/Doorstop Books, 1990). She was joint-winner of The Poetry Business Pamphlet Competition 1989, and the Peterloo Poets Afro-Caribbean/Asian prize 1990.

RICHARD MCKANE has translated the work of several Russian and Turkish poets into English, including Anna Akhmatova, Osip Mandelstam and Nazim Hikmet. A collection of his own poems, *The Rose of the World*, is being published in 1991 by Gnosis Press, New York and Diamond Press, London.

FELICITY NAPIER was born in 1943, grew up in Gloucestershire, and has lived and travelled extensively in the Far East. She worked for six years in the art world before becoming a glass engraver, and has recently obtained a first class honours degree in Modern Arts from Kingston Polytechnic. She now lives in Twickenham with her family, and divides her time between writing poetry and short fiction and taking creative writing groups at local day-centres. Her poems have appeared in magazines and anthologies, and on television and radio, and she has won the Leek and Redcliffe poetry competitions. Some of the poems in this anthology first appeared in *Encounter*, *The Spectator*, *Ambit*, *New Statesman*, *No Holds Barred* (The Women's Press, 1985), and *Fire the Sun* (Longman, 1989).

BIBHU PADHI was born in 1951 and has spent his entire life in Cuttack, an ancient town in the eastern Indian state of Orissa, where he teaches English at Ravenshaw College. His poems and translations of Oriya poetry have appeared in *Encounter*, *Orbis*, *Outposts*, *Poetry Wales*, *Poetry* (Chicago), *Southwest Review*, *TriQuarterly*, *Queen's Quarterly*, *2PLUS2*, and *The New Criterion* which first printed 'Migratory Cranes Near Lake Chilka'. His first book of poems *Going to the Temple* was published in 1988 by Indus Publishing Company, New Delhi; Peepal Tree Press are publishing a second in 1991. He has also written a critical study of D.H. Lawrence, and (with his wife, Minakshi Padhi) a reference book on Indian philosophy and religion.

WILLIAM PALMER was born 1945 and was educated at various schools in England and Wales. After a bewildering variety of jobs he is now a full-time writer, whose poems and stories have appeared in many magazines, including *London Magazine*, *Poetry Review*, *Stand Magazine* and the *TLS*, in which some of the poems printed here were first published, and *Critical Quarterly* and *The Rialto*, as well as being broadcast on Radio 3 and 4. His first novel *The Good Republic* was published by Secker and Warburg in 1990. He lives in the Midlands with his wife and daughter.

PETRA REGENT was born in London in 1957, grew up in Fife, Scotland, and began writing poetry while reading Zoology at Oxford. After spending a year as a journalist on a local London newspaper, she went to Sulawesi on an expedition to create a reserve in the Indonesian rainforest. She now works as a producer and scriptwriter on wildlife films in London. Acknowledgements for poems here are due to *Envisage* and *The Gregory Awards 1980* (Secker and Warburg, 1980). Other poems have appeared in *Outposts* and *The Bark & the Bite*.

OKTAY RIFAT (1914–1988) was one of the leaders of a revolutionary movement in Turkish poetry in the early 40s, which rejected the complex forms of the poetry of the past for new rhythms and Brechtian simplicity. His work includes translations from Greek and Latin, plays, political satire, experiments in surrealist poetry, and lyric poetry which celebrates his love of the Mediterranean landscape. He was also a painter.

VALERIE THORNTON was born in 1954 in Glasgow, and was educated in Stirling and at Glasgow University. Five none too happy years teaching English were followed by five years of temporary jobs, including film festival work and copy-writing. She now teaches creative writing to adults and writes subtitles for Ceefax. She has published poems and short stories in several magazines and anthologies, including *Lines Review*, *New Writing Scotland*, *Glasgow Herald*, and *Fresh Oceans* (Stramullion, 1989), in which some of the poems here first appeared. She is about to publish a book on window boxes, and is currently working on a screenplay.

GERARD WOODWARD was born in North London in 1961 and educated at Falmouth School of Art and the London School of Economics. He has worked on building sites, in shops, hospitals, factories, and warehouses, and as community worker, freelance artist and waiter. His poetry has appeared in many magazines including the *TLS*, *Encounter*, *Poetry Review*, *The Spectator* and *Stand Magazine*, which first published some of the poems printed here. In 1989 he received a major Eric Gregory award. A pamphlet, *The Unwriter & Other Poems*, was published by Sycamore Press in 1989 and a full collection of his poems is due from Chatto & Windus in 1991.